INTRODUCTION TO

IQBAL

S. A. VAHID, M.A.

Qadeem Press

Qadeem Press

Qadeem Press Edition
Breathing Life into Forgotten Pages
www.qadeempress.com

Originally Published by Pakistan Publication, Karachi
Reprinted by Qadeem Press in 2025

Find our titles on your favourite online bookstore using the keyword 'Qadeem Press'

Contents

ONE

Biographical Sketch

FOR people migrating from the State of Jammu and Kashmir, either to escape political oppression or to seek fresh grounds for their adventurous spirits, Sialkot. a town situated in the Punjab, on the border of the State, has for centuries provided the first halting place. Waves after waves of emigrants from Jammu and Kashmir have passed through this town, some never to return to ancestral home, others to return after having amassed enough to live on for the rest of their lives. In most cases the emigrant families, after staying for a short time in Sialkot, moved on to places further south in the Indo-Pakistan sub-continent, where these gifted people made a mark in every walk of life—trade, commerce, law and politics; but in many cases the families were reluctant to go far from ancestral homes and so stayed on in Sialkot. Thus Sialkot town, which is today a great centre of industries in Pakistan, contains a large number of Kashmiri families. Iqbal's grandfather, Muhammad Rafiq, left the ancestral home in the village of Looehar and came to settle in Sialkot along with his three brothers. It was in this town that Iqbal was born on 22nd February, 1873 (Zilhajja 24, 1289 A. H) in a middle class family. At the time of his birth, the busy town, as may be supposed, was quite heedless of what was then passing in the corner of that low thick-beamed house in one of its streets. His father, Nur Muhammad, who was at the time of Iqbal's birth, carrying on business in Sialkot, was a deeply religious man who attached great importance to spiritual values.

When Iqbal grew up and the question of education began to worry the family. Nur Muhammad, following the established practice, put him in a mosque where he learnt Quran. after finishing which he was put in an elementary school. In the school Iqbal shone himself, winning scholarships and prizes. It was about this time that Iqbal attracted the attention of a great friend of his father, Shamsul-Ulema Meer Hasan, who was an erudite scholar, great savant and an inspiring teacher. Meer Hasan was so impressed by the perspicacity of his young pupil's intellect that he encouraged him in every way. Iqbal was, in fact, a precocious child. This will probably startle many readers, especially if they have adopted the current notion that precocity is a sign of disease, and that marvellous children are necessarily evanescent fruits which never ripen: early blossoms which whither early. It may help to remove confusion on the subject if we bear in mind that men distinguish themselves by *receptive* capacity and by *creative* capacity, they learn and they invent or create. In men of the highest class, like Goethe and Iqbal, these qualities are united. Iqbal's precocity was nothing abnormal. It was the activity of a mind at once greatly receptive and greatly creative. As a receptive mind Iqbal read omnivorously and excelled at his studies. As a productive mind he began writing verses while still at school. When Moulvi Meer Hasan came to know about these he not only encouraged Iqbal to continue writing verses but even advised him to write in Urdu in preference to the local dialect.

In his childhood, scanty as the details are which enable us to reconstruct it, we see the main features of the man. The most noticeable feature is his many-sidedness. Seldom has a boy exhibited such variety of faculty, we see him as an orderly, inquisitive, deliberative child, and one who thinks for himself. He gave his parents no tremulous anxiety as to what will become of him. He was very much master of himself.

After passing his matriculation, Iqbal joined the Scotch Mission College for his Intermediate studies. It was about this time that Iqbal sent some of his verses, mostly lyrics, to the well-known Urdu poet Dagh for correction. Although these lyrics lacked the breadth and maturity of later work, after correcting some poems Dagh wrote back to Iqbal that his poems did not need any revision. It may be mentioned that Dagh lived long enough to see young Iqbal acquire countrywide popularity and he often used to refer with pride to the fact that at one time he had corrected Iqbal's poems. Iqbal passed his first University examination from the Scotch Mission College in 1895 and then migrated to Lahore for higher studies, and to lay, as he hoped, the solid foundation of a future professorship. He had brought with him a wild uneasy spirit struggling towards the light. He was now aged 22. His features were large and liberally cut, the brow was lofty and massive and from beneath it shone deep-set penetrating lustrous brown eyes of great attraction. The slightly aquiline nose was large and well cut. The mouth was full with a short arched upper lip, very sensitive and expressive. The chin and jaw were boldly proportioned and the head rested on a muscular neck. In stature he was rather above the middle size. His frame was strong, muscular, yet sensitive.

In Lahore

About this time Lahore was fast developing into a great intellectual centre. Urdu was replacing Persian and to encourage the development of Urdu several societies were sponsored and were doing great work in Lahore. Some of these societies occasionally organised poetical symposium.

About this time a literary society was formed in Lahore whose membership included some well-known literary figures of the time. Iqbal recited his well-known poem on the Himalayas at one of the meetings of the society. This poem was published in the *Makhzan* for April, 1901, a newly started Urdu Journal. This served to introduce Iqbal to a wide circle all over the country. In the beginning the publication of his poems was confined to *Makhzan* but as his popularity and fame spread, other papers and journals also approached him for permission to publish his poems and very often succeeded in getting.

The first important poem Iqbal read in a large gathering was at the annual meeting of the Anjuman-i-Himayat-i-Islam of Lahore in

1899. The poem was *Nalal-i-Yatimee.* Next year he recited *An Orphan's Address to the Id Crescent* at the same meeting.

At Lahore Iqbal came under the influence of Sir Thomas Arnold, an influence which in its potency can be well compared with that of Moulvi Meer Hasan at Sialkot. It did not take Sir Thomas Arnold long to discover Iqbal's gifts of heart and intellect, and with his sympathetic insight he soon succeeded in piercing the shell that obscured a most beautiful individuality. While Moulvi Meer Hasan's influence and guidance had given Iqbal a deep insight into the humanistic foundations of Muslim Culture, Sir Thomas Arnold's company introduced him to all that is best and noblest in Western thought, and at the same time initiated him into the modern methods of critical studies.

Iqbal obtained his degree of M.A. in philosophy in 1897 under the guidance of Sir Thomas Arnold. During this period Iqbal was lucky to have various influences, the most powerful being that of his parents at home. His father was an honest God-fearing man with great love of learning who had many scholarly friends, who gathered for studies or discussions at his business premises. Iqbal often attended these discussions, listening quietly. These attendances could not but create in the mind of the inquisitive youth a love of learning and research. His mother was a quiet, old-fashioned lady, very religious in her outlook. Iqbal was deeply attached to her and her influence in moulding the character of her young son can only be judged by the tribute paid to her by Iqbal in the poem he wrote on her death.

From early youth Iqbal developed a complex personality characterised by antithesis which, inspite of later maturity and development, continued to retain its complexity. But the traits that Iqbal developed in childhood, as a result of home and outside influences, remained with him all his life. These were his sense of integrity, passion for justice and love of freedom.

From the Oriental College Iqbal moved to the Government

College, Lahore as Reader in Philosophy. During this period he stayed near Bhati Gate and it was about this time that Ali Baksh, his faithful servant and companion, joined him in what proved to be life-long partnership.

This was also a period of intensive studies and prolific production not confined to poetry. Iqbal's position as a poet of renown in the Indo-Pakistan sub-continent was fully established. He also got his first book, which happens to be the first book on Economics in Urdu language, published about his time.

In Europe

As advised by Sir Thomas Arnold, Iqbal went to Europe for higher studies in 1905. On his way to Bombay he visited the Dargah of Khawaja Nizamuddin in Delhi and paid his homage to the two great poets that lie buried there—Amir Khusrau and Ghalib.

In Europe, Iqbal began to see the larger horizon of things and to move in spacious realms. He stayed there for three years, and these years played a great part in the development of his thought. He was admitted as an advanced student of philosophy in Cambridge and he joined Lincoln's Inn for the Bar. For his degree in Cambridge he wrote a thesis 'Development of Metephysics in Persia'. After he had put in a short residence and acquired a knowledge of the German language, Munich University conferred on him the degree of Ph.D. for the same thesis. He was called to the Bar in 1908. During his stay in England, Iqbal was forced with a great conflict. He began wondering whether he should adopt a life of action or reflection. There was such a dearth of man of action in the country that Iqbal very nearly adopted a life of action, and so he wanted to give up writing poetry. But he was pursuaded by his friend, Sir Abdul Qadir, and his teacher, Sir Thomas Arnold, not to do so. It was better so for the world. Imagine the loss humanity would have sustained if the noble, majestic and inspiring poetry of Iqbal had not added to its glory and lustre. But his admiration for a life of action and struggle became more pronounced during his stay in Europe.

Iqbal's outlook on life underwent another change during his stay in England: he got an utter dislike for narrow and selfish nationalism and racialism which were the root-cause of most political troubles in Europe.

He delivered a series of lectures on Islam in England, the first of which was delivered at Caxton Hall and a summary of which was reproduced in all the leading papers of the country.

After having got his degree from Cambridge, his doctorate from Munich and having been called to the Bar, Iqbal returned home in August, 1908.

Subsequently, he joined the Government College as a part-time Professor of Philosophy and English literature. He was allowed to practise law. But after sometime he resigned the professorship and concentrated on law.

He composed some epoch-making poems about this time like *Shikwa* and *Jawab-i-Shikwa*, but the great event was the publication of his poem—*Asrar-i-Khudi* in 1915. This book created a storm in the dovecots of the pseudo-mystics, but nothing was going to keep Iqbal back from preaching his gospel. His attack on Hafiz as representing those who preached ascetic inaction was strongly resented and several replies in prose and verse were published. But these effusions of pseudo-artists and pseudo-mystics were in due course consigned to oblivion, and Iqbal lived to see the great popularity achieved all over the world by his great poem. So far as Iqbal himself was concerned, from now onwards there was complete accord in his thought, the goal was clear and the future lines of his work were well-defined. The task that Iqbal had set himself of reforming a moribund society steeped in moral decadence was gigantic. But Iqbal was not to be dismayed by these considerations. Still the overflow of senseless criticism that Iqbal had to endure about this great work *Asrar-i-Khudi*, and that too not only from the indiscriminating multitude but from people who stood near him, left him depressed and made him realise the loneliness of his position. He prayed for a sympathetic companion in these words:

> I beg of Thy grace a sympathising friend,
> An adept in the mysteries of my nature
> How long shall I wait for one to share my grief ?
> How long must I search for a confidant.

But he went on his way in silence and severity. *Asrar-i-Khudi* was followed by *Rumuz-i-Bekhudi*. The poem was completed in 1917, but was not published till the following year. In *Asrar* and *Rumuz* the poet delivered the message that he had for mankind. The former treats of the doctrine of the individual self; the latter deals with the problems which face the society and society's collective self, in relation to the individual and the environment.

Meanwhile his collection of early Urdu poems was published under the name *Bang-i-Dira*. This was followed by *Payam-i-Mashriq* or *The Message of the East*. The book is a collection of miscellaneous verses in Persian and was written in response to Goethe's *West-Ostlicher Divan*. *Payam-i-Mashriq* was followed two years later by *Zabur-i-Ajam* (Persian Pslams). The book contains mystic, vitalising and ennobling verses. *Zabur-i-Ajam* was followed by *Javid Namah* which can be regarded as Iqbal's *magnumn opus*. It is an Oriental *Divine Comedy*, and in it Iqbal has beautifully expressed his thoughts on the various problems that confront men in daily life. The poem will rank among the world's classics.

After finishing the *Javid Namah* Iqbal turned to Urdu again and published a collection of Urdu poems *Bal-i-Jibrail* in 1935, and another collection *Zarb-i-Kalim* in 1936. In 1934 he had also published a Persian poem *Musafir*. Another Persian poem *Pas chai bayad kard* appeared in 1936. The final collection of his poems containing poems in Urdu as well as Persian and called *Armughan-i-Hijaz*, appeared posthumously.

Though the fame of Iqbal rests mainly on his poetry, it must not be forgotten that he has left us three books in prose out of which "*The Reconstruction of Religious Thought in Islam*" deserves special mention. This book contains six lectures delivered by Iqbal at Madras, Hyderabad and Aligarh. Iqbal's philosophy, presented to us in other writings only in dispersed poetic gleams or in diffused living glow, is here presented in the form of a thesis. The gospel of Iqbal, that is the fullest expression of what he regarded as his spiritual message to his time will be best learned from these lectures. The collection was published by the Oxford University Press, and it was mainly due to this publication that Iqbal was selected by the Oxford University for the Rhodes Lectureship, and was invited to deliver a series of lectures at Oxford. He accepted the invitation but the engagement had to be cancelled owing to his failing health.

Iqbal's place in literature is certainly amongst the greatest in the world, both as a poet and as a prose-writer, but that is certainly not his only value. His contribution to human thought is as great, and so his biographers will be faced with a two-fold task: to trace the development of his literary genius and to trace the growth of his thought. It will be quite easy to trace the development of his literary genius as his literary productions are before us and they provide enough material for this work. But the study of the development of his thought will not be so easy as there is not enough material with us which can throw sufficient light on the mental conflict through which he passed. We have his article in the *Indian Antiquary* of Bombay, which shows that Iqbal was reflecting on the conception of a superman or a perfect man as early as 1902, long before he had studied any works of Nietzsche. His early poems breathed of stress and struggle and this belief in the importance of struggle was transformed into a faith during his stay in the West. His respect for human personality was also an article of faith with him. This respect made him appreciate the importance of freedom for every society. But he realised the baneful effects of narrow nationalism only after his visit to the West. This much is clear. But we have no conclusive evidence as to when he actually thought out his philosophy of ego. It is clear that he developed this philosophy as a result of his reaction to the doctrine of *Wahdat-al-Wajud* which is based on pantheism. We have to determine as to when he began realising the harmful effects of this doctrine on human progress. We have the following letters from Dr. McTaggart written in 1920 which will throw some light on the subject: "I am writing to tell you with how much pleasure I have been reading your poems *Secrets of the Self*. Have you not changed your position very much? Surely in the days when we used to talk philosophy together you were much more of a pantheist and mystic. For my own part, I adhere to my own belief that selves are the ultimate reality, but as to their true content and their true good my position is as it was, that it is to be found in eternity and not in time, and in love rather than in action". From this letter it is clear that Iqbal believed in pantheistic Sufism when he left Cambridge in 1908. His poem *Asrar-i-Khudi*, in which he deals with the philosophy of ego, was published in 1915. It must have been written in 1914. This shows that Iqbal must have developed his philosophy of ego which forms the corner-stone of his entire philosophy between 1908 and 1914. A reference to his philosophy is also contained in his Urdu poem *Shama aur Shair* which was published in 1912. Thus the real period of conflict is reduced to the period between the years 1908 and 1912. An exhaustive study of the development of Iqbal's thought in this period will be found to be illuminating and interesting. This study must be undertaken before the material available gets destroyed. We have the statement of his servant Ali Baksh that on the day Iqbal resigned his professorship in the Government College he told him: "Ali Baksh, I have a message for my people and it could not possibly be conveyed if I remained in service; so I had to resign the service and I hope that now I will be able to carry out my wish". This happened sometime in 1911. Is it possible that at the time of resignation Iqbal had already resolved the conflict? Only detailed research can furnish an answer to this question.

While writing poetry Iqbal's versatile genius allowed him to devote attention to politics also. In 1927 his friends pursuaded him to stand for the Punjab Legislative Assembly, the Provincial Parliament, to which he was elected. In 1927 he gave evidence before the

Simon Commission which was visiting the sub-continent in order to suggest a scheme of political reforms for the Indo-Pakistan sub-continent. In 1930 he was selected to preside at the annual session of the Muslim League. It was in his presidential address to the Muslim League at Allahabad that Iqbal elaborated his scheme for the solution of the political deadlock in the Indo-Pakistan sub-continent. In 1931 and 1932 he attended the Round Table Conference which met in London to frame a constitution for the sub-continent. In 1932 he presided at the annual session of the Muslim Conference, and delivered a thought-provoking address. He was for many years president of the Punjab Mulim League. What impelled Iqbal to take part in politics was his love of freedom. He believed that human personality could deveolp only in an atmosphere of freedom, and so he wanted elementary human rights assured to all people irrespective of nationality, creed or class.

As Educationist

It has already been mentioned that Iqbal started his career as a teacher in the Oriental College, Lahore. When he came to Lahore his ambition was to become a professor at a College. Thus he started as an educationist, and an educationist he remained all his life.

In Lahore he taught English Literature and Philosophy. In London he taught Arabic Literature for a short time. But even after the close of his association with the education department he continued to exercise a great influence over the affairs of the Punjab University by working on various bodies connected with it. For years he was Dean of the Faculty of Oriental Studies and Chairman of the Department of Philosophy. He was closely connected with the Islamia College, Lahore for years. In 1933 he was invited by the Government of Afghanistan to visit Kabul and advise them on reorganization of Kabul University. He took great interest in the Jamia-Millia of Delhi and was always ready to help its promoters in every possible way. Thus it will be seen that he continued to take interest in education all his life, and his contribution to educational progress of the sub-continent was substantial.

But it must be remembered that Iqbal's real service to the cause of education is not to be measured so much by what he actually did for it from time to time in official or non-official capacities, but should be estimated on the basis of the ideals of education he placed before us in his poems. This aspect of the question has been dealt with by Mr. K.G. Saiyidain in an admirable monograph '*Iqbal's Educational Philosophy*.' Mr. Saiyidain observes in this monograph:—

"The emergence of an outstanding creative thinker, who has a distinct message to impart and new values to present before world, is a phenomenon of the greatest interest for the educationist and the more his ideas catch the imagination, the understanding and the enthusiasm of his contemporaries, the greater must be his influence as an educative force".

As A Lawyer

Iqbal practised as a lawyer from 1908 to 1934, when due to ill-health he had to give up the profession. Law is reputed to be a jealous mistress and it is very difficult to attain eminence unless one is prepared to give it undivided attention and time. Iqbal had so many interests that it was impossible for him to give undivided attention to law. Still it must be remembered that while Goethe failed as a lawyer and had to give up the profession, Iqbal practised law all his life, and whatever detractors may say he earned his living from the profession. That a man with such multifarious activities could not possibly give his undivided attention to the legal profession was foregone, but that in spite of these activities he attained a fair degree of eminence is a credit even to his versatile genius. Apart from the heavy toll his various activities as a poet, writer, thinker, politician and educationist levied on his time we have to remember that Iqbal never wanted to make a fortune out of law. His aim was to earn enough to live on. He brought to his profession a profound knowledge of law and a great conscientiousness and thoroughness. These qualities were enough to enable him to climb the heights in the profession if he had only chosen to do so.

The Last Phase

Iqbal developed kidney trouble in 1924; for its treatment he wanted to visit Vienna, but some friends advised him to consult the well-known physician Hakim Abdul Wahab Ansari, popularly known as Hakim Nabina, the blind physician. Treatment by Hakim Abdul Wahab cured him of his trouble. After this he kept fairly good health till the beginning of 1934, when he developed loss of voice. Complications ensued later on. Every possible treatment was tried in Lahore, Delhi and Bhopal but without success. In 1935 he was invited to Oxford as Rhodes lecturer but finally ill-health compelled him to decline the invitation. In 1937 he developed cataract in his eye. In spite of periods of comparative good health the last phase was embittered by constant ill-health. But so far as his creative activities were concerned this period was the most productive. Till the last Iqbal kept in touch with every important question of the day, and he took great interest in the controversies going on.

Iqbal was a profound student of the Quran. He had devoted a whole lifetime to its study, and he wanted to write a book on it, and had collected a large number of books for this purpose. He was thinking of calling the book "The Reconstruction of Muslim Jurisprudence". But failing health compelled him to give up the idea of writing this book which he had already started. It is most unfortunate that Iqbal's profound and erudite scholarship and lifelong study of the Quran could not assume a tangible form for the benefit of future generations. About this time Iqbal was also thinking of writing a prose poem in English language which he wanted to call "The Book of a Forgotten Prophet", but this work also never assumed any definite form on paper. As regards poetry he continued composing verses till the very end. The last poem was dictated only a few days before his death.

His illness took a serious turn on 25th March 1938, and in spite of the best medical aid and careful nursing of his friends he breathed his last in the early hours of 21st April. Half an hour before his death he recited the following verses:—

The departed melody may or may not recur,
The Zephyr from Hijaz may or may not blow;
The days of this Faqir have come to an end,
Another seer may or may not arrive.

Although his illness was long and protracted, the end was sudden and very peaceful. On his death-bed he presented a picture of peace and composure. It seemed as if he was just resting after finishing his life's work.

On his death-bed Iqbal reminded one of his well-known lines:—

I tell you the sign of a *Momin*
When death comes there is a smile on his lips.

This reminds one of the remarks made by Goethe to Eckermann: "The thought of death leaves me perfectly calm, for I hold a firm belief that the soul is a being of absolutely indestructible nature and continues active to all eternity".

He was given a funeral which kings might envy and his remains were buried near the gate of the historic Badshahi Mosque in Lahore, late in the evening, in the presence of thousands of mourners.

A few days before his death he had told his brother:

"I am a Muslim and I am not afraid to die".

There are not many clear cases in the history of mankind of a man born with a mission, of a life irresistibly but unconsciously moving along a pre-ordained path. To attain his mission Iqbal spurned prizes that the world covets. He realized the fundamental truth that man's personality can endure and develop only in an atmosphere of freedom and it was in preaching fervently to his people this forgotten truism that his greatness lay.

Iqbal bewilders us by the complexity and the many-sidedness of his genius. To get a glimpse of the pattern of mind and being that underlay the phenoman that was Iqbal one has to study him closely. Only then one can realise the great miracle he has worked: he has moulded the minds of the present generation of Pakistanis.

When gathering my chattels I forsook this world
All and sundry said: "We knew him well",
Forsooth none knew about this wanderer—
What he said? Whom he addressed and whence he hailed?

TWO

His Poetry

ACCORDING to Iqbal the true aim of poetry, as of all arts, is to make human life rich and beautiful, and poetry that fails to do this has failed in its great mission. If art does not contribute to the fullness and exuberance of life and fails to provide guidance for humanity in the various problems that baffle it, it is meaningless. To Iqbal art represents man's attempt to grasp the realities of life, and for him great artists cannot be conceived to have girded themselves to their great efforts merely to provide intellectual toys for human entertainment. According to Iqbal the keynote of all art must be a desire to impress upon mankind those great truths which alone can bring about the amelioration of human race. The main object of his poetic art is to come to the help of his readers in the struggle of life. And to achieve this he sings of life. Describing art Iqbal says:

> O discerning ones, thirst for knowledge is welcome.
> But what is in art that fails to grasp the reality of things.
> The object of all art is to attain warmth of life immortal.
> What good is existence for a breath or two like a spark.
> Without a miracle nations cannot rise.
> What is art without the striking power of Moses's staff!

Iqbal has no patience with people who talk of "Art for Art's sake". According to him Art must be for life. Heaven had made him a great artist, but he was not a mere decorative artist. The aim of his art was to provide succour and guidance to humanity in its onward march. He utilised his great art to utter those truths which alone can bring salvation to mankind, and therein lies its true significance for humanity. And it is this feature which tends to make the appeal of his art universal. For Iqbal the two powerful impulses to artistic expression are his faith in human capacity for limitless development and man's unique position in the universe; and both these impulses, serve to impart an unparalleled charm to his poetry.

Iqbal tried his hand at every kind of verse, except the dramatic. He wrote lyric, philosophic, epic, mataphysical, descriptive, and satiric verse. This vast range of poetry needs wide and varied sensibility seldom met with, except in the greatest poets of the world.

Iqbal started his poetical career by writing lyrical poetry in the form of '*ghazals*', and today his lyrics are perhaps better known than any other kind of poetry written by him. The magical cadence and musical ecstasy of Iqbal's lyrics have made them universally popular. He turns our simple experiences of life into passionate experiences, and communicates these in such vivid and moving imagery that it cannot fail to strike a sympathetic response. In his songs even the abstruse notions of philosophy and religion are set free from their academic isolation and become a part of the common life of men. This could be accomplished only by a great artist. By formulating a life of ceaseless striving and discountenancing all view of life which advocated renunciation and self-annihilation Iqbal has actually widened the scope of lyric poetry so far as Urdu and Persian languages are concerned. If man is not to donascetic's sackcloth, but is to live an active life with his fellow-men, there will be many more occasions for the play of his emotions—joy over success, grief over disappointments, exultation in effort. Life, according to Iqbal, is nothing but a progressive succession of fresh ends, purposes and values. This in itself ensures an un-ending succession of those thrills of souls, those rapturous glows of feeling, which provide the very substance which makes the finest lyrical poetry.

In Urdu and Persian poetry *ghazal* represents the finest kind of lyric. But *ghazal* generally suffers from the lack of unity of themes, because the poet does not confine himself to one emotion. Iqbal's emotional intensity is remarkable and he had a keen ear for melody and harmony. He instinctively selects words which serve to enhance the rhythm of his language. In order to illustrate this we have only to refer to two of his well-known *ghazals*.

O world of earth, wind, water ! are you the
　　Secret brought to light, or I ?
Are you the continent of that which lies
　　concealed from sight, or I ?
The night of pain and passion and of troubling
　　men call life—are you
Its dawn, or I ? are you the call to prayer which
　　ends that night, or I ?
To whose revealing make such haste the evening
　　and the dawn? Are you
Upon the shoulder of the world the heavy load
　　bound tight, or I ?
You are a pinch of dust, and blind; I am a
　　pinch of dust that feels—
Are you the flowing stream that lifts from
　　life's dry fields their blight, or I ?

(*Translation by V. G. Kiernan*).

——0000——

Thine is the hawk upon the wing
And thine the thrush sweet-carolling,
Thine is the light and joy of life
And thine its fire and baneful strife.

Thou gavest me a heart awake
And, through the world my way to take,
A little dust—a moon forlorn
Upon a night-dark litter borne.

My every thought from thee doth start,
Whether on lip or in the heart;
Whether the pearl be brought from sea,
Or left enfoundered, 'tis of thee.

I am the selfsame cloud of dust
Swept idly as the wind doth lust;
Tulip, and springtime's scattered dew,
Thou art their sole creator too.

Thou art the painter; thy design
Inspires and moves this brush of mine;
Thy hands the living world adorn,
And shape the ages yet unborn.

Much sorrow in my heart I had
That by the tongue could not be said:
Love, lovelessness, troth, treachery—
All things alike are sprung of thee.

(*Translation by Prof. A. J. Arberry*).

A recurrent theme in Iqbal's lyrical verse is his conception of beauty and love. While Iqbal saw beauty in everything except the really ignoble and mean, the beauty which appealed to him most was the beauty of power and perfection. Beauty is a mental experience and not a quality of things, it is relative in its appeal. Iqbal sees manifestation of beauty in everything that is powerful and perfect. This conception of beauty has imparted to his poems that robust vitality and manliness which is singularly lacking in most of the Oriental lyric poetry.

How long the veil of eve and dawn
About thy beauty shall be drawn?
Thy cheek display: make whole to me
This incomplete epiphany.

O glad consuming! rapture fine!
Thyself wouldst beg of me for wine
If unto thee I did relate
The intoxication of my state

I added to the song of life
The counterpoint of fiery strife;
Scatter the dew that quenches drowth
Into the tulip's thirsty mouth.

Mind searched the volume thro' and thro',
Love found at once the subtle clue;
The clever bird will ever gain
Beneath the snare the hidden grain.

Where is the song, and he that sung?
Words are a lyre pretence has strung;
I draw towards the camel-train
The erring beast without a rein.

In riddles yet I spake, forsooth;
Now is the time for naked truth;
Do thou declare, where I shall lead
My fellow-travellers in their need.

(*Translation by Professor A. J. Arberry*).

While Iqbal has sung of all human emotions, the theme of Love is paramount. Great emphasis is laid on the part Love plays in the development of human personality and character, and the term is used in a very wide sense. As we have seen, Iqbal's philosophy of lifeinsists on ceaseless activity and insatiable yearning, and this is part of his doctrine of Love. But though Love leads to restlessness, it is this very rest- lessness which makes life worth living.

All that in life I love the best
Is the sweet fever of thy quest;
The way is like an adder's sting,
Be not to thee my wayfaring.

Lo, Gabriel with naked heart
Out of love's bosom doth depart,
Hopeful to catch a spark of fire
From the vast flame of thy desire.

Anon I rend my veil in twain,
Yearning the vision to attain;
Anon with unavailing sight
I veil myself before thy light.

Whether in quest of thee I go,
Or at the last myself I know,
Intellect, heart, sight—all astray
Blindly they wander on thy way.

I was a seedling of thy mead;
Sprinkle thy dew upon my head;
The blossom's heart will quicken, yet
No drop shall lack the rivulet.

(*Translation by Professor A. J. Arberry*).

Iqbal's poetic genius was so comprehensive that even in his lyrics he displayed great versatility. He could write poems whose perfection resides in their spontaneity and he could also produce poems whose perfection lies in their art. Yet again he could write poems in which both spontaneity and artistry could blend efficiently and harmoniously. This synthesis makes Iqbal one of the finest lyrical poets of the world.

The days are ended
Of winter long;
The branches quiver
With living song.

The breeze in beauty
Arrays the rose
As from the river
It gently blows.

The tulip's lantern
In desert bare
Is fanned to brightness
By the spring air.

Sad, mid the roses,
My heart doth dwell,
Yea, from the meadow
Flees the gazelle;

A little eases
With grief and pain
Or like a hill-stream
Laments again.

Lest my heart's passion
May softer grow,
Not to the trusty
I'll tell my woe.

(*Translation by Professor A. J. Arberry*).

Iqbal spent his childhood in Sialkot a town along the foothills of the outer Himalayas. Amongst these beautiful surroundings he developed very early a love of Nature, which inspired some noble poetry. One of his early popular poems was on '*The Himalayas*', which he had then only seen from a distance. There is often a personal note in his treatment of Nature; for example describing the advent of spring he says:

Arise! for on hills and dales
The spring has arrived
Mad in singing are nightingales
Cuckoos, partridges, and quails,

Along the banks of the brook
Have sprung roses and the poppy,
Come out and see.
Arise! for on hills and dales
The spring has arrived!

There is another lovely poem on Kashmir, the country of hi. origin, which he loved deeply:

Alight in Kashmir and behold the mountains, the hills and the dales,
Behold the green grass all over and gardens full of poppies.
Feel spring breeze in wave after wave, see birds in myriads,
The wood pigeons and the starlins in pairs on the poplars.
The poppies have sprouted from the dust, ripples play on the stream surface,
Behold the dust full of sparks and water wrinkled by ripples!

The azure sky overhead, the air charged with joy!
Even the birds will not stay in their nests!
And behold yonder the mountain stream leaping,
Conquering obstructions, swaying, and crawling;
See it jumping over or slipping by obstacles and then eddying on,
Rushing forth in spite of many a curve and twist!
Just behold, O Saqi, bright-faced!
How the stream conveys the message of life!

In the beginning, like Wordsworth, Iqbal was a pantheist in his treatment of Nature. He says:

In each thing glows some spark of beauty immortal
Mankind has speech, and buds with all hues dazzle
A secret union lurks with dispersal
One are the firefly's glitter, the flower's sweet phial

(*Translations by V. G. Kiernan*).

But later Iqbal's views regarding pantheism underwent a profound change. He began regarding each object as endowed with a distinct personality. Thus Iqbal's treatment of Nature shows a wide sensibility and an extensive range.

With his incisive humour and penetrating wit Iqbal is as at home in satire as in lyrical verse. His satire is characterised by smoothness of verse, lucidity of style, and straightforwardness of manner.

The pride, pedantry, and stupidity of the religious leaders are assailed with invective and humour in the following lines:

The true religion has sunk lower than irreligiousness,
For the *Mulla*, though religious, is busy branding people irreligious.
Our dew appears the ocean to us—
To him our ocean seems but dew.
He appreciates not the wisdom of the Prophet's teachings,
His firmament is dark being starless.
Short-sighted, crude and an aimless wanderer,
His harangues but serve to disrupt the community.
The religion of the *Kafir* consists of planning for earnest endeavour,
The religion of the *Mulla* is creating trouble in the name of God.

In another poem the *Mulla* is described with sardonic humour:

I was present there and could not hold my tongue
When God ordained the *Mulla* to Paradise,
Submissively I uttered: "Forgive me,
He will not care for houri, wine and verdant fields.
Paradise is not the place to bicker, argue and quarrel,
And quibbling and wrangling form the very nature of this man.
Throwing mud on people and faiths is his vocation,
And in Paradise there is no mosque, no church, no fire-temple."

No study of Iqbal's poetry can be complete without a reference to his longer peoms, known in Urdu and Persian as *mathnawis*. There are critics who maintain that a long poem is really a contradiction in terms, because according to them, poetry is essentially the language of excitement, and as exitement is always of brief duration, there can be no such thing as a long poem. While the force of this argument cannot be totally denied it must be said that this criticism of long poems is to a certain extent based on a misunderstanding of the true nature of poetry. While the universal appeal of short poems, mostly lyrical, cannot be denied, it must be admitted that long poems, by giving the poet an apportunity for sustained effort, provide a truer test of his art. While it will be wrong to suggest that the excellence of a poem depends upon its length, it can safely be said that the long poem can be successfully composed only by a great poet.

Among Iqbal's longer poems (*Mathnawis*), the first two *Asrar-i-Khudi* and *Ramuz-i-Bekhudi* are metaphysical and ethical. A shorter *mathnawi*, *Gulshan-i-Raz Jadid*, is philosophical and the last, *Javid Namah* is epic.

Asrar-i-Khudi was first published in 1915. It describes the fundamental principles affecting the development of human personality. This poem attracted world-wide attention owing to its translation in English by Professor R. A. Nicholson of Cambridge. In his introduction to the translation, Professor Nicholson remarked:

> "The artistic quality of the poem is remarkable when we consider that its language is not the author's own. I have done my best to preserve as much of this as a literal translation would allow. Many passages of the original are poetry of the kind, that once read, is not easily forgotten."

Hailing the advent of a fully developed personality or ego, Iqbal says:—

Appear, O rider of Destiny
Appear, O light of the dark realm of Change!

Silence the noise of the nations,
Imparadise our ears with thy music!
Arise and tune the harp of brotherhood,
Give us back the cup of the wine of love!
Bring once more days of peace to the world
Give a message of peace to them that such battle!
Mankind are the cornfield, and thou the harvest.
Thou art the goal of Life's caravan.

(*Translation by R. A. Nicholson*).

In *Rumuz-i-Bekhudi* Iqbal has described the basic principles on which the organisation of ideal human society should be based. The poem is a detailed practical blue-print for the Islamic State, on its ideology, its structure, its social ethics and its mission among other human societies. This is also a poem of great artistic value and an English translation by Arberry is already in the Press.

Gulshan-i-Raz Jadid deals with a number of mystical problems; the poet sets himself nine questions and then goes on to give replies to them.

But Iqbal's *magnum opus* is *Javid Namah.* In this poem the poet, accompanied by Rumi, who is to him what Virgil is to Dante, visits the various stellar spheres and meets historical personalities who, in discussion, elucidate eternal truths. The poet first visits the Moon. Here Rumi introduces him to a Hindu sage Jehan Dost (Vishwamitra). Rumi tells Jehan Dost that today for mankind the way to progress lies through the synthesis of Eastern and Western cultures. East has been concentrating on the spiritual and neglecting the material, while West has been concentrating on the material and neglecting the spiritual.

The East saw God but failed to see the world of matter,
The West got embroiled in the world and neglected God.

Later on the poet goes over to the Valley of Yarghmeed, where he comes across the tablets of Buddha, Zaroaster, Christ and Muhammad, four spiritual leaders and teachers of mankind. Then he is transported to Mercury where he meets the Muslim leaders, Jamaluddin Afghani and Said Halim Pasha. The poet tells Afghani the mistakes Eastern nations are making in Westernising themselves. Said Halim Pasha compares the East and the West and points out that the salvation of mankind lies in the synthesis of the two civilizations.

Afghani exhorts the poet to tell the Communists that without faith and religion all their progress will come to naught.

From Mercury the poet is transported to Venus and from Venus to Mars, and thence to Jupiter. Here he meets the poet Ghalib, the poetess Tahira and the mystic Mansur Hallaj. The poet then reaches Saturn where he meets those mean souls who have been guilty of treason against their own countries and ideals.

From Saturn the poet reaches the Region beyond Heaven, and here the first person he meets is Nietzsche, who tried all his life to understand the nature of God, but failed completely, because in his attempt she relied on intellect alone. After seeing Nietzsche the poet flies to a Higher Region where he gets a glimpse of the palace of Sharfun-Nisa, the daughter of Abdus Samad, the Governor of the Punjab. Later he meets the saint Syed Ali Hamdani and the poet Ghani of Kashmir. The poet refers to the sale of Kashmir by the British to Gulab Singh in the following lines.

> On breeze! if you pass by Geneva
> Convey this message of ours to the League of Nations:
> They sold peasants, crops, rivers and gardens
> In short, sold a whole nation, and that too so cheap!

The poet then meets the Hindu poet Bharatrihari and three Eastern potentates—Nadir Shah, Ahmad Shah Abdali and Tipu Sultan. Ahmad Shah refers to the growing tendency in Eastern countries to adopt Western methods of living and styles of dress, and remarks on the futility of this blind imitation.

It is not possible to attempt here a critical analysis of *Javid Namah*, but some of its outstanding features deserve mention. The most noticeable feature is the marvellous variety of effect produced by the introduction of lyrical interludes. These lyrical interludes serve to heighten the effect of variety by providing changes in rhythm and style at intervals, without any laboured effort. The highest truths are uttered in a language which is admirably natural and inevitable. In *Javid Namah* the language used by each character reflects his or her personality. The very sound of the words suggests the character of the person talking. Another remarkable feature of the poem is the great sympathy with which the poet treats his characters, irrespective of their religious or political views. In fact, the only persons for whom the poet displays any feelings of disgust and contempt are those who proved traitors to their countries and ideals. Even when describing these traitors the language used in the poem is particularly free from roughness.

This brief survey of Iqbal's poetry will show that all those who turn to it will find in it a fusion of art and thought all his own and which places him among the few greatest poets of the world.

THREE

Iqbal as Thinker

AMIR Shakaib Arselan once remarked that Iqbal was the greatest thinker produced by Islam during the last one thousand years. Iqbal is a philosopher and a poet and in him philosophy and poetry seem to be indissolubly blended as they have seldom been in other thinkers. Iqbal's pilosophy is essentially the philosophy of the Self. For him the Self is a veritable reality. As the reality of the Self has been denied by the pantheists who regard the world of phenomena as non-existent and unreal, Iqbal started by assailing those who believed in the doctrine of *Wahadat-al-Wajud*—which is based on pantheism. This doctrine led one to believe in God as immanent and regarded the whole world merely as an emanation. Thus a pantheistic deity was substituted for the personal and transcendent God of Islam. The system of Sufiism, built on the basis of *Wahadat-al-Wajud*, led groups of Islamic peoples to spurn a life of activity and exertion. Ideas based on this doctrine sapped the energies of the people. They encouraged men to run away from the difficulties of life instead of grappling with them, and engendered a feeling of other-worldliness which led people to take delight in spending all their time in thinking of the joys of Nirvana. Life came to be regarded as a mere illusion, and nothing in life seemed worth striving for. Iqbal assailed this doctrine by laying emphasis on the reality of Self. According to him we can directly see that the Self is real and existent. The Self is revealed as the centre of all our activity and action. It is the core of our personality and is to be named as ego. Ego as revealed by intuition is essentially directive, free and immortal. The ego is essentially appreciative; it appreciates itself in its own activity. But this appreciation would come to it only if its activity is purposeful. There would be no appreciation without achievement and no achievement without purpose. The ego always moves in some direction. Thus essentially it is directive in its nature. The ego develops into a strong purposeful personality by desires and aspirations. Desires presuppose an environment. Hence the development, nay even the life of the ego, depends upon its having established some connection with an objective reality: the world, the society, the Ultimate Reality. The Self cannot grow in isolation. Hence the ego has to confront a non-ego at every step. This leads to an important question: Is the activity of the ego determined by its own self or by environment? In other words is the ego free or not? The mere fact of purposive activity in our life shows that we are not impelled by forces that may push us from behind. We constantly move towards the future. Moreover freedom can be directly intuited. Freedom thus is not a mere inference. Man, though living in an environment which is provided for him, has the power to re-shape the environment according to his will. His freedom is manifested in his action. If however his freedom is obstructed by his environment he has the power to devote himself to his own self. Obstruction and hindrance therefore only serve to sharpen the insight and the power of the ego. This serves to make man self-conscious and helps him to find in the deep recesses of his being a free cause and a free personality.

The ego is not only free: it is also immortal. Action confers on us the intuition that the ego is immortal. We can have a peep into our immortality even in this life of ours and that through intuition. But according to Iqbal immortality is "not ours by right. It is to be achieved by personal effort."

Thus it will be seen that in the first place the human ego has to struggle with its environment and to conquer it. By this conquest it attains freedom and approaches God which is the Most Free Individual. In the second place the ego has to maintain a constant state of tension by maintaining desires and purpose, and thereby it attains immortality. The basis of this philosophy is a strong faith in the evolution of man on two planes: personal freedom and personal immortality. How is this evolution to be attained? By fortifying personality. Man must follow all that tends to fortify personality and must avoid all that is likely to weaken it. Thus it will be seen that it is of the highest importance to study the factors which fortify the human ego. According to Iqbal these factors are:

(*i*) Love.

(*ii*) *Faqr*: which can be best described by the expression "supreme indifference to the rewards the world has to offer."

(*iii*) Courage.

(*iv*) Tolerance.

(*v*) *Kasb-i-Halal*: which can be best translated as living on lawful earnings.

(*vi*) Taking part in original and creative activities.

The following remarks will serve to elucidate the nature of these factors:

(*i*) *Love.*—For Iqbal Love connotes far more than the bringer of a purely individual joy. To him Love is the regenerating spirit of the universe, the spirit that should cut the Gordion knot of man's perplexities, and provide an antidote to all human vices. In a letter to Professor Nicholson, Iqbal writes: "This word is used in a very wide sense and means the desire to assimilate, to absorb. Its highest form is the creation of values and ideals and the endeavour to realise them. Love individualises the lover as well as the beloved."

The nearest approach to Iqbal's conception of Love is perhaps that of the great Oriental mystic poet, Maulana Rumi.

Iqbal has described the connection between Love and Ego in these lines:

> The luminous point whose name is the Self,
> Is the life-spark beneath our dust.
> By love it is made more lasting,
> More living, more burning, more glowing.
> Transmute thy handful of earth into gold,
> Kiss the threshold of a Perfect Man.
> From the wine of Love spring many spiritual qualities:
> Amongst the attributes of Love is blind devotion.
> Be a lover constant in devotion to the beloved,
> That thou mayst cast thy noose and capture God.

(*Translation by R. A. Nicholson*)

(*ii*) *Faqr*.— By *Faqr* Iqbal means the disdain for the rewards which this world, or the next, has to offer, and which the majority of mankind covet. According to Iqbal, the term means an attitude of complete detachment from and superiority to one's material possessions. As such it provides a shield against the temptations which beset one in the world.

(*iii*) *Courage*.— Without courage, physical and moral, it is impossible for man to achieve anything really important in this world. Progress means encountering obstacles which only serve to draw the best out of those possessing courage. It is only the weaker ones who succumb to obstacles. Courage does not consist merely in facing manly physical danger. There is greater courage in not losing faith in one's standard of values when things go wrong.

(*iv*) *Tolerance*.—Tolerance for other people's views and manners represents the strength of a high order and its cultivation cannot but be beneficial to the ego. Iqbal has remarked "The principle of the ego-sustaining deed is respect for the ego in myself as well as in others."

(*v*) *Kasb-i-Halal.*—This is a very expressive and inclusive phras with such wide application as to provide guidance for human condu in all spheres of human activity. Translated literally, the phras means 'lawful earning'. But according to Iqbal the phrase has a wid meaning, and means acquiring things and ideas solely through one personal effort and struggle. It thus prescribes for ego a life c active effort and struggle, and totally excludes all thought of sel renunciation.

(*vi*) *Creative and original activity.*—We have seen that by extollin 'Kasb-i-Halal' Iqbal enjoins a life of activity if the ego is to attain pro per development. Now he goes further and lays down that all acti vity must be creative and original if the ego is to be sustained an fortified. Great stress is laid by Iqbal on creativeness and he refers to the Quran which expressly recognises creators besides God.

As opposed to the forces which tend to fortify personality, there are influences which weaken the ego. These are given below:—

(*i*) Fear
(*ii*) Beggary (*Swal*)
(*iii*) Slavery
(*iv*) Pride of extraction.

We will deal with all these influences briefly.

(*i*) *Fear.*—Fear produces all sorts of unhealthy and abnormal emotional developments in man which warp his nature and stultify his moral growth. The abnormal man, the bully, the coward, the tyrant and the dictator,—has the origin of his abnormality in suppressed fear. It is essential that the ego must overcome the paralysing effect of fear, before it can attain full growth.

(*ii*) *Beggary* (*Swal*).—Iqbal does not use this term in the restricted sense in which it is generally used to denote begging. According to him all that is achieved without personal effort comes under *swal*. The son of a rich man who inherits his father's wealth is a beggar, so is the person who borrows his ideas from others. And *swal* in every form is inimical to the development of ego, and must be avoided.

(*iii*) *Slavery*.—Of all the institutions ever designed by the ingenuity of man for the exploitation of his fellow beings, none is more degrading than slavery. Slavery distorts character, warps human nature and lowers man to the level of a beast, and naturally enough it tends to weaken the human ego. As such it must be eradicated if the human ego is to develop properly. Even political subjugation and economic serfdom should be banned if mankind is to attain moral and spiritual stature.

(*iv*) *Nasab-parasti*.—The phrase means the pride in one's stock or extraction. This must be discouraged as it tends to create barriers between man and man, based on considerations other than those of intrinsic worth. To take pride in such extraneous considerations as one's family, nation or race is not a healthy feeling and it is bound to retard the development of an ego.

By encouraging influences which fortify the ego, and by avoiding those which lead to its weakening, the ego grows from strength to strength. But we have to bear in mind that the ego can develop fully only in association with other egos and not in isolation. As a matter of fact the ego has to work in co-operation with others in mutual interests. This adjustment of personal activity to social good is mutually beneficial because the individual cannot achieve his highest possibilities except by identifying himself with social purpose. This means that the individual ego has to live and work in a society. So we have to decide what kind of society is needed for the free development of the ego and what kind of society provides the greatest scope for the developed ego. Before determining the nature of this ideal society we have to lay down optimum relations between society and individual. On the one hand there are individualists who regard the development of the individual as the supreme end of life's process and the State as merely an instrument for this development. On the other hand there are Hegelians who regard the State as a super-personal entity whose strength is far more important than the rights of the individual. Between these two extremes Iqbal takes a balanced view and maintains that the growth of a full and free personality is impossible except where it draws its spiritual sustenance from the culture of the group to which it belongs. On the other hand, the group, in its own interests owes a duty to the individual and so interferes with his development as little as possible, and only when common good demands it. For such an ideal society Iqbal has laid down eight essential requirements:—

(*i*) It must be based on spiritual considerations like monotheism.
(*ii*) It must centre round inspired leadership or prophethood.
(*iii*) It must possess a code for its guidance.
(*iv*) It needs a centre.
(*v*) It must have a clear goal towards which the whole community should strive.
(*vi*) It must gain supremacy over the forces of nature.
(*vii*) The communal or collective ego must be developed in the same way as the individual ego is developed.
(*viii*) It must safeguard maternity.

Now we shall deal with these requirements in detail.

(*i*) *Monotheism.*—Any society which fails to recognise the fundamental brotherhood of mankind is doomed to failure. Basing any human society on considerations of race, colour, creed or geography is like putting up an imposing building with insecure foundations. If society is to be based on a secure basis, that basis must be spiritual—too deep-rooted to be affected by any adverse influences. This spiritual basis is provided by the principle of monotheism which gives us a foundation of world unity by admitting the basic principle that all mankind represents one brotherhood. The principle of monotheism, viewed psychologically, seeks to restore to a torn and divided world its integral unity. It provides for all members of the society unity of thought and unity of action. Hence all great religions have insisted on this doctrine. "Thou shalt have no other gods before me. Thou shalt not make unto thee any graven image......Thou shalt not bow down thyself to them, nor serve them: for I the Lord thy God am a Jealous God...." (Exod. xx, 3-5). The Quran says:

> God forgiveth not
> That equals should be set up
> With Him; but He forgiveth
> Anything else, to whom
> He pleaseth; to set up equals with God
> Is to devise a sin
> Most heinous indeed. —*IV*: 48.

The belief in one God provides an effective antidote to all those reactionary forces which exploit hatred and provoke antagonism. It provides a psychological basis for society by restoring the essential unity of mankind, and by insisting that all mankind represents one brotherhood bound together by a spiritual connection. It is only such ideas that can act as a unifying force and break down the division of mankind into warring tribes and antagonistic camps.

> That which leads to unison in a hundred individuals
> Is but a secret from the secrets of *Tawhid.*
> Religion, wisdom and law are all its effects,
> Power, strength and supremacy originate from it.
> Its influence exalts the slaves,
> And virtually creates a new species out of them
> Within it fear and doubt depart, spirit of action revives,
> And the eye sees the very secret of the Universes!

(*ii*) *Prophethood.*—The part played by prophets in the evolution of humanity cannot be over-estimated, and the devotion that men have always displayed towards all great prophets gives us a measure of mankind's recognition of the debt it owes to those inspired leaders. Loyalty to prophets has always been a source of strength to their people; and for the Muslims the great and remarkable personality of the Prophet provides a focus where all loyalties converge and all disrupting tendencies disappear. Thus faith in prophethood or inspired leadership provides the second important corner-stone for the structure of the ideal society.

> On prophethood is based our existence on this earth,
> From prophethood are derived our religion, our code.
> The Prophet moulded hundred thousands of us into one,
> So that various parts were inseparably welded into each other.
> From prophethood we attained unity of tune;
> It imparted to us the unity of breath and the unity of objective.

(*iii*) *The Quranic Code.*—A society must have a code to guide it during periods of uncertainty and trouble. Amidst the fluctuations of values which cause the truths and certainties of one generation to appear as superstitions and empty conventions in the eyes of a succeeding generation, the code imparts stability to the life of the people. This code serves as an anchor-sheet in this world of shifting values, and when the community, faced with the turmoils of life, begins to lose faith in itself and in its standard of values, the code serves as a beacon of light directing the community to safe waters. Without a proper code the communal life is sure to end in confusion. For the Muslims the code is provided by the Quran.

(*iv*) *Centre.*—Every society needs a centre from which all its cultural and social activities will radiate. These activities provide the society with its life-blood, and the centre functions as a heart, providing fresh and invigorating blood to the distant limbs. So long as the centre is there to provide this life-giving blood, the whole body will function properly and without dislocation. For the Muslims this centre is provided by Mecca. It was a further extension of this theory of a 'cognizable centre' in space, which helped the formation of the philosophic concept of Pakistan.

(*v*) *Objective.*—To attain real solidarity every group or community must have a well-defined goal or objective towards the attainment of which all its activities must be guided. This ideal serves as a land-mark to guide the community when, owing to decadence, there is disunity of purpose among the rank and file. For the Muslims this objective is the propagation of the doctrine of the unity of God or monotheism, and a nobler objective is hard to think of ! Others may have such mundane objectives as the conquest of land or the attainment of political power and supremacy, but these are not capable of stimulating the life of high endeavour and unselfishness which only a great spiritual objective is capable of doing.

(*vi*) *Conquest of the forces of nature.*—To fortify his personality every individual and eventually the society must acquire mastery over environment, that is to say, attain sway over the forces of nature by developing the study of sciences. This means the development of a scientific outlook in man who, thereby, begins probing into the mysteries of Nature. While all this is necessary for an individual, for a social community it is a matter of life and death. The West owes its supremacy to its development of physical resources and study of natural phenomena, and one of the main causes of Eastern decadence is the neglect of physical sciences.

(*vii*) *Development of the communal ego.*—In order to attain stability and prosperity the society must develop its collective ego and this is rendered possible by conserving its traditions. To see the important part played by traditions in the life of a group, one has only to look at the history of the Jews. This small community has been harassed in all countries for centuries, and at times the prospects of its survival have looked very slender indeed; still the Jews have weathered all storms and survived. This is because through all their trials and tribulations the Jews have remained faithful to their traditions.

During the period of prosperity every community creates certain healthy traditions, and in the gloomy days of adversity the community can do no better than to stick to these traditions till there is a turn of the tide.

(*viii*) *Maternity.*—Maternity, in Iqbal's conception of the social structure of the ideal human society, symbolises all that is best in the woman, all that she has to offer to humanity in her chaste, steadfast, unassuming manner in humanity's march of evolution.

Thus it will be seen that Iqbal, in his philosophy of the ego, has not only provided a complete scheme for the development of individuals but has also prescribed the essentials of the society, which on the one hand will help the development of the individual, and on the other provide the best scope for the creative unfolding of man's individuality. But there are two important questions which still remain: the nature of the universe surrounding man and the nature of Ultimate Reality. We have seen that according to Iqbal the life of the ego consists in the mutual contention of the ego and the environment—the ego invading the environment and the environment counter-invading the ego. Thus the existence of the external world or environment is involved in the life of the ego, and it is obvious that the external world exists and is real, but the question arises as to what is the exact nature of the external world. Iqbal tries to determine the nature of the external world by having recourse to analogy. On the analogy of the self, it may be maintained that the physical world, too, exists in time, but time is the peculiar possession of a self only. The physical world must accordingly be regarded as a unique self. If the nature of the universe is that of the self, it follows that it is life and is in a state of constant flux and change. In the universe there is constant activity, action and movement, and like all life the universe is free, creative and essentially original. The universe, therefore, is a constantly growing universe which is bursting and burgeoning at every instant. It is a constantly progressing, self-generating, and self-evolving universe whose inner possibilities of growth and evolution will never know any limits. In short the world is a free, dynamic process and not a static existence.

Iqbal regards the Ultimate Ego also as of the nature of the self. But the Ultimate Ego does not lie apart from the universe as if separated by a space lying between Him and ourselves. This leads us to the conclusion that the Ultimate Self is not transcendent as conceived by anthropomorphic theists. He is immanent as He holds the finite egos in its own self without obliterating their existence. On the analogy of the self, the Ultimate Reality has an ego-hood, that is to say He has consciousness of His own "I-am-ness" like us, but His "I-am-ness" does not lie within the grasp of our experience. Thus the Ultimate Ego is transcendent also. In short the Ultimate Reality is transcendent as well as immanent and yet neither one nor the other. But an emphasis on immanence would lead to a dissolution of the human ego in the Infinite and this would be like giving up the reality of the self which is the corner-stone of Iqbal's thought and philosophy. Hence Iqbal emphasises the transcendence of the Ultimate Ego rather than His immanence. Insistence on transcendence serves two purposes: on the one hand it emphasises the existence of the finite ego and on the other it brings to light the individuality and ego-hood of the Infinite.

We have given above, in brief outline, the gist of Iqbal's philosophy of the ego, but actually there is no phase of human activity in which Iqbal does not provide us with guidance. It is not possible to deal with Iqbal's philosophy in general here. But enough has been said to show that Iqbal's philosophy, preaching the gospel of self-reverence, brings a message of hope and cheer to humanity, distracted and tramelled by its own greed and passion for aggrandizement.

FOUR

Iqbal as Architect of Pakistan

ON 14th August, 1947 there came into existence a new State—Pakistan. This State has a population of 76 millions. It is the largest Muslim State and the fifth largest State in the world. Iqbal was the first man to conceive this State and he played a momentous part in its creation, although he did not live long enough to see its actual creation. Before appreciating the part played by Iqbal in the establishment of this new State it is necessary to understand the historical background of Muslim connection with the sub-continent. While the first Muslim contacts with the sub-continent through the Arab sailors and merchants started earlier, the first Muslim invasion of the sub-continent took place in 712 under the leadership of a young intrepid general, Mohammad Bin Qasim. This invasion resulted in the conquest of Sind, and the majority of the inhabitants of Sind have remained Muslim until the present day.

This first invasion was followed by invasions from the north by Sultan Mahmood of Ghazni, who invaded the sub-continent seventeen times between 999 and 1025. Mahmood succeeded in annexing the Punjab. In course of time the house of Ghazni was supplanted by the dynasty of Ghor. Shahabuddin Ghori, a scion of this dynasty, conquered the Kingdom of Delhi in 1192. From 1192 to 1526 five Turkish or Afghan dynasties ruled at Delhi, the first Sultan being Qutbuddin. After the decay of Turkish power under the Tughlaqs the representative Muslim dynastics in the sub-continent were no longer in Delhi, but were represented by the Sultans of Bengal, Jaunpur, Gujrat and Malwa.

The Hindu society which was politically disorganised, morally decadent, and socially degenerate when it came in contact with Islam began a process of recovery soon after the establishment of the Muslim power on the sub-continent. But at this time a phenomenon of singular importance occurred. Hinduism, so noted for its power of absorbing other ideological, sociological and religious systems, failed to do that with Islam. As a Hindu historian has remarked:—

"The main social result of the introduction of Islam as a religion into India was the division of society on a vertical basis. Before the thirteenth century, Hindu society was divided horizontally, and neither Buddhism nor Jainism affected this division. They were not unassimilable elements and fitted in easily with the existing divisions. Islam, on the other hand, split Indian society into two sections from top to bottom and what has now come to be known in the phraseology of today as two separate nations, came into being from the beginning. It was two parallel societies vertically established on the same soil. At all stages they were different and hardly any social communication or intermingling of life existed between them. There was of course a continuous process of conversion from Hinduism to Islam, but also a continuous strengthening of the Hindu social body, both by the rise of new doctrines and sects as well as by a defensive feeling of security."

K. M. Pannikar: A Survey of Indian History pp. 162

The Moghuls succeeded the Turco-Afghans in 1526, and their rule lasted from 1526 to 1707 with a short break. Babar was the first ruler of the family, but Akbar and Aurangzeb were the great kings of this dynasty. Akbar subdued the greater part of the sub-continent and ruled over Afghanistan also. He obtained the support of local chieftains by confirming them in their estates and by marriage alliances. Aurangzeb was the last of the great Moghuls. He spent much of his life fighting for the expansion of the empire and in trying to restore the pristine purity of Islamic way of life.

The death of Aurangzeb was followed by the disintegration of the Moghul Empire. The Marathas appeared in Central and Western

India. Delhi was sacked by Nadir Shah, and the strength of the British, French and Dutch settlements developed. A number of Muslim successor states also grew about this time. But as soon as British East India Company had disposed of its European rivals it inexorably absorbed both Hindu and Muslim states, so much so that after the Mutiny in 1857 Hyderabad was the only big Muslim State in existence. The political and economic downfall of the Muslims that started soon after Aurangzeb's death reached its culmination in the nineteenth century. The Muslims now found themselves deprived of all power and authority in the country. The period of extreme Muslim depression was between 1833 and 1864. English replaced Persian as the official language in 1833, and as Muslims were not quick in learning English they lost their traditional places in the police, courts of law, magistracy and revenue offices. The new Code of Macaulay displaced Muslim criminal law which had been applied in Northern India for many centuries. Anglo-Muslim law amended the Shariat law. Annexation of Oudh by the East India Company meant the loss of everything in the north of the sub-continent and Islam, after six hundred years of power, found itself reduced to a position which was altogether intolerable. The reaction was of many kinds. Religious re-orientation, Wahabi puritarism, cultural non-co-operation, even open hostility. Syed Ahmad Shaheed and Ismail Shaheed organised groups of gallant fighters for heroic crescentades against the Sikhs and the British. Even the uprising for independence in 1857 was a last desperate bid to throw off the British yoke. To make matters worse till 1864 the attitude of looking upon the Muslims as opposed to British authority was accepted as the true basis of British policy in the sub-continent. For the Muslims the situation was truly desperate and Islam had now to find a new policy or die. The man who saw this most clearly was Syed Ahmad the founder of Aligarh Movement. The Aligarh Movement is the central factor of Islamic renaissance in the sub-continent and was the first step towards the integration of Islam. The new century saw other developments. The Aligarh movement was split into two: the older leaders supporting the policy of Syed Ahmad unconcerned with Islam outside the sub-continent, the younger pursuing a frankly anti-British policy on the ground that Britain was ranged against Islam everywhere in the world.

In 1907 when the question of political reforms became urgent and Minto-Morley scheme was on the anvil the British Government decided to introduce separate electorates for the Muslims. This secured for the Muslims a certain amount of protection.

From the beginning of the century the Muslims were confused and perplexed and were siding with the Hindus and the British in turn. Both wanted to exploit them. They were afraid that with the introduction of democratic rule they were bound to be swamped by resurgent Hinduism.

Morley-Minto reforms were followed by Montagu-Chelmsford Reforms in 1917. The treatment accorded to the Muslims by the Ministries under the diarchy in most of the Provinces was neither fair nor equitable. This left them baffled and frustrated. In the wake of political coercion economic boycott and other disabilities there followed communal riots. Dr. Ambedkar, in a careful analysis of communal disturbances between 1920 and 1940 has described the period as one of Civil war between Hindus and Muslims, interrupted by brief periods of armed peace. In Cawnpore in March 1931 he estimates that between 400 and 500 persons were killed; in Bombay Province between February 1929 and April 1938 there were 210 days of rioting, causing 560 deaths and 4,500 injuries. In Bengal between 1922 and 1927 there were 35,000 women abducted. As the Simon Commission noted the communal riots were "a manifestation of the anxieties and ambitions aroused in both the communities by the prospect of India's political future. So long as authority was firmly established in British hands and self-government was not thought of, Hindu-Muslim rivalry was confined within a narrow field...... The coming of the Reforms and the anticipation of what may follow have given new point to Hindu-Muslim competition. The one community naturally lays claims to the rights of a majority, and realises upon its greater qualifications of better education and greater wealth; the other is all the more determined on these accounts to secure effective protection for its members and does not forget that it represents the previous conquerors of the country".

Simon Report Vol. 1, p. 29.

In a series of All Parties Conferences and unity Conferences attempts were made to draft an agreed Constitution for the sub-continent, but without success. It was in this atmosphere that Iqbal was called upon to preside at the annual session of the Muslim League held in Allahabad in 1930. In his presidential address Iqbal stated:—

"Communalism in its higher aspect, then, is indispensable to the formation of a harmonious whole in a country like India. The units of Indian society are not territorial as in European countries. India is a continent of human groups belonging to different races, speaking different languages and professing different religions. Their behaviour is not at all determined by a common race-consciousness. Even the Hindus do not form a homogeneous group. The principle of European democracy cannot be applied to India without recognising the fact of communal groups. The Muslim demand for the creation of a Muslim India within India is, therefore, perfectly justified. The resolution of the All-Parties Muslim Conference at Delhi, is, to my mind, wholly inspired by this noble ideal of a harmonious whole which, instead of stifling the respective individualities of its component wholes, affords them chances of fully working out the possibilities that may be latent in them. And I have no doubt that this House will emphatically endorse the Muslim demands embodied in this resolution. Personally, I would go further than the demands embodied in it. I would like to see the Punjab, North-West Frontier Province, Sind and Baluchistan amalgamated into a single State. Self-Government within the British Empire or without the British Empire, the formation of a consolidated North-West Indian Muslim State appears to me to be the final destiny of the Muslims, at least of North-West India. The proposal was put forward before the Nehru Committee. They rejected it on the ground that, if carried into effect, it would give a very unwieldy State. This is true in so far as the area is concerned; in point of population the State contemplated by the proposal would be much less than some of the present Indian provinces. The exclusion of Ambala Division and perhaps of some districts where non-Muslims predominate, will make it less extensive and more Muslim in population so that the exclusion suggested will enable this consolidated State to give a more effective protection to non-Muslim minorities within its area. The idea need not alarm the Hindus or the British. India is the greatest Muslim country in the world. The life of Islam as a cultural force in this country very largely depends on its centralisation in a specified territory. This centralisation of the most living portion of the Muslims of India, whose military and police service has, notwithstanding unfair treatment from the British, made the British rule possible in this country, will eventually solve the problem of India as well as of Asia. It will intensify their sense of responsibility and deepen their patriotic feeling. Thus possessing full opportunity of development within the body-politic of India, the North-West Indian Muslims will prove the best defenders of India against a foreign invasion, be the invasion one of ideas or of bayonets".

"Nor should the Hindus fear that the creation of autonomous Muslim States will mean the introduction of a kind of religious rule in such States. I have already indicated to you the meaning of the word religion as applied to Islam. The truth is that Islam is not a church. It is a State conceived as a contractual organism long before Rousseau ever thought of such a thing, and animated by an ethical ideal which regards man not as an earth-rooted creature, defined by this or that portion of the earth but as a spiritual being understood in terms of social mechanism, and possessing rights and duties as a living factor in that mechanism. The charter of a Muslim State can be judged from what the 'Times of India' pointed out some time ago in a leader on the Indian Banking Enquiry Committee. 'In ancient India', the paper points out, 'the State framed laws regulating the rates of interests, but in Muslim times, although Islam clearly forbids the realization of interest on money loaned, Indian Muslim

State imposed no restrictions on such rates'. I therefore demand the formation of a consolidated Muslim State in the best interests of India and Islam. For India it means security and peace resulting from an internal balance of power; for Islam an opportunity to rid itself of the stamp that Arabian imperialism was forced to give it, to mobilize its law, its education, its culture, and to bring them into closer contact with its own original spirit and with the spirit of modern times".

Few thought at the time that Iqbal's foresight would lead to the creation of the independent and sovereign state of Pakistan.

Presiding over the session of the Muslim Conference in 1932 Iqbal elaborated the programme for the Muslims of the sub-continent if they desired to lead an honourable life free to follow their ideals:

"Those phenomena, however, are merely premonitions of a coming storm, which is likely to sweep over the whole of India and the rest of Asia. This is the inevitable outcome of a wholly political civilization which has looked upon man as a thing to be exploited and not as a personality to be developed and enlarged by purely cultural forces. The peoples of Asia are bound to rise against the acquisitive economy which the West has developed and imposed on the nations of the East. Asia cannot comprehend modern Western capitalism with its undisciplined individualism. The faith which you represent recognises the worth of the individual, and disciplines him to give away his all to the service of God and man. Its possibilities are not yet exhausted. It can still create a new world where the social rank of man is not determined by his caste or colour, or the amount of dividend he earns, but by the kind of life he lives; where the poor tax the rich, where human society is founded not on the equality of stomachs but on the equality of spirits, where an untouchable can marry the daughter of a king, where private ownership is a trust and where capital cannot be allowed to accumulate so as to dominate the real producer of wealth. This superb idealism of your faith, however, needs emancipation from the medieval fancies of theologians and legists. Spiritually we are living in a prison-house of thoughts and emotions which during the course of centuries we have woven round ourselves. And be it further said to the shame of us—men of older generation—that we have failed to equip the younger generation for the economic, political and even religious crises that the present age is likely to bring. The whole community needs a complete overhauling of its present mentality in order that it may again become capable of feeling the urge of fresh desires and ideals. The Indian Muslim has long ceased to explore the depths of his inner life. The result is that he has ceased to live in the full glow and colour of life, and is consequently in danger of an unmanly compromise with forces which, he is made to think, he cannot vanquish in open conflict. He who desires to change an unfavourable environment must undergo a complete transformation of his inner being. God changeth not the condition of a people until they themselves take the initiative to change their condition by constantly illuminating the zone of their daily activity in the light of a definite ideal. Nothing can be achieved without a firm faith in the independence of one's own inner life. This faith alone keeps a people's eye fixed on their goal and saves them from perpetual vacillation. The lesson that past experience has brought to you must be taken to heart. Expect nothing from any side. Concentrate your ego on yourself alone, and ripen your clay into real manhood if you wish to see your aspirations realized. Mussolini's maxim was: 'He who has steel has bread'. I venture to modify it a bit and say: 'He who is steel has everything'. Be hard and work hard. This is the whole secret of individual and collective life. Our ideal is well defined. It is to win in the coming constitution, a position for Islam which may bring her opportunities to fulfil her destiny in this country. It is necessary in the light of this ideal to rouse the progressive forces of the community and to organise their hitherto dormant energies. The flame of life cannot be borrowed from others; it must be kindled in the temple of one's own soul. This requires earnest preparation and a relatively permanent programme. What then shall be our future programme? I am inclined to think that it should be partly political, partly cultural. I venture to offer a few suggestions for your consideration."

In a letter to Quaid-i-Azam Jinnah, Iqbal wrote on 28th May, 1931:

"........After a long and careful study of Islamic Law I have come to the conclusion that if this system of Law is properly understood and applied, at least the right to subsistence is secured to everybody. But the enforcement and development of the Shariat of Islam is impossible in this country without a free Muslim State or States. This has been my honest conviction for many years and I still believe this to be the only way to solve the problem of bread for Muslims as well as to secure a peaceful India. If such a thing is impossible in India, the only other alternative is a civil war which as a matter of fact has been going on for some time in the shape of Hindu-Muslim riots. I fear that in certain parts of the country, *e.g.*, N.-W. India, Palestine may be repeated. Also the insertion of Jawaharlal's socialism into the body-politic of Hinduism is likely to cause much bloodshed among the Hindus themselves. The issue between social democracy and Brahmanism is not dissimilar to the one between Brahmanism and Buddhism. Whether the fate of socialism will be the same as the fate of Buddhism in India I cannot say. But it is clear to my mind that if Hinduism accepts social democracy it must necessarily cease to be Hinduism. For Islam the acceptance of social democracy in some suitable form and consistent with the legal principles of Islam is not a resolution but a return to the original purity of Islam. The modern problems therefore are far more easy to solve for the Muslims than for the Hindus. But as I have said above in order to make it possible for Muslim India to solve these problems it is necessary to redistribute the country and to provide one or more Muslim states with absolute majorities. Don't you think that the time for such a demand has already arrived. Perhaps this is the best reply you can give to the atheistic socialism of Jawaharlal Nehru.

"Anyhow I have given you my own thoughts in the hope that you will give them serious consideration either in your address or in the discussions of the coming session of the League. Muslim India hopes that at this serious juncture your genius will discover some way out of our present difficulties."

In a letter to Quaid-i-Azam Jinnah, Iqbal wrote in 1937:

"You are the only Muslim in India today to whom the community has a right to look up for safe guidance through the storm which is coming to North-West India, and perhaps to the whole of India." Further on he wrote in the same letter:—

"A separate federation of Muslim provinces re-formed on the lines I have suggested above is the only course by which we can secure a peaceful India and save Muslims from the domination of non-Muslims. Why should not the Muslims of North-West India and Bengal be considered as nations entitled to self-determination just as other nations in India and outside India are."

In the Foreword to Iqbal's letters, the Quaid-i-Azam wrote in 1943.

"It was a great achievement for Muslim League that its lead came to be acknowledged by both the majority and minority provinces. Sir Muhammad Iqbal played a very conspicuous part, though at the time not revealed to public, in bringing about this consummation........His views were substantially in consonance with my own and had finally led me to the same conclusions as a result of careful examination and study of the constitutional problems facing India, and found expression in due course in the united will of Muslim India as adumbrated in the Lahore resolution of the All-India Muslim League, popularly known as the "Pakistan Resolution" passed on 23rd March, 1940."

No greater tribute could be paid to the architect of Pakistan, and the tribute assumes special significance when it comes from the great leader who actually achieved a free homeland for 80 millions people distracted and distraught by political subjugation and economic emasculation, who could think of no solution for their difficulties until Iqbal came to show them the light.

Thus it will be seen that not only Iqbal saw in Pakistan the only solution of the political, social and economic ills of the Muslims living in the sub-continent, he also chose the man who alone could achieve it and furthermore he pursuaded Quaid-i-Azam Jinnah to work for it. The people of Pakistan owe a debt to Iqbal which can only be paid to some extent by working ceaselessly for the ideal which he cherished. Iqbal enunciated these ideals in his address to the Muslim League in 1930 in the following words:—

"One lesson I have learnt from the history of Muslims. At critical moments in their history it is Islam that has saved Muslims and not *vice versa.* If to-day you focus your vision on Islam and seek inspiration from the ever-vitalising idea embodied in it, you will be only reassembling your scattered forces, regaining your lost integrity, and thereby saving yourself from total destruction. One of the profoundest verses in the Holy Quran teaches us that the birth and rebirth of the whole of humanity is like the birth and rebirth of a single individual. Why cannot you who, as a people, can well claim to be the first practical exponents of this superb conception of humanity, live and move and have your being as a single individual? I do not wish to mystify anybody when I say that things in India are not what they appear to be. The meaning of this, however, will dawn upon you only when you have achieved a real collective ego to look at them. In the words of the Quran, Hold fast to yourself; no one who erreth can hurt you, provided you are well guided. (5 : 104)"

There is no other instance in the history of mankind of a poet and a philosopher working such a miracle in shaping the destiny of his people.

FIVE

The Reconstruction of Religious Thought in Islam

IN the previous chapters we have described the great contributions Iqbal made in the realms of poetry and philosophy. We have also dealt with the important part he played in the sphere of politics leading to the establishment of the greatest Muslim State in the world. Attention has already been drawn to the brilliant versatility of Iqbal's genius which is so well illustrated by his work in such different spheres as poetry, philosophy and politics. While it is not possible to deal here with his work in fields other than those mentioned above his momentous and epoch-making contributions to the religious thought deserve mention in view of their far-reaching importance and unparalleled originality in the history of Islamic thought. Iqbal was born and brought up in a Muslim family, which was deeply devoted to religion. Even in his childhood he used to listen with rapt attention to the religious discussions that his father used to carry on with other scholars in Sialkot. His father encouraged him and sometimes guided him in the study of the Quran. The religious influence that his mother exercised on him in her own quiet way was no less profound. These early influences, although considerably modified by his subsequent extensive studies and original thinking, had permanent effect on Iqbal who continued to be a profound student of religion all his life, and in his studies he brought such original thought and intensive effort that his studies have assumed considerable importance for all interested in religion.

The work of early *mutakallimin** had introduced rationalism in Islam, which received further impetus due to the study of Greek

*It is not easy to define a *mutakallim*. He represents a scholastic and a rationalist combined.

philosophy by Muslim scholars. But unfortunately reactionar tendencies soon asserted themselves and all growth in the religiou thought of Islam came to a standstill nearly five hundred years ag only to be revived by that savant and religious scholar Shah Wa Ullah of Delhi. The pioneer efforts of Shah Wali Ullah to rationalis Islam were kept up to a certain extent by his sons and grandsons but no sustained effort to rationalise religions thought in Islam wa made until Sir Syed Ahmad Khan, the great leader of the Muslims in the Indo-Pakistan sub-continent, took up this work. Unfortunatel Sir Syed Ahmad Khan was considerably handicapped in his grea task by the fact that his knowledge of Western thought and sciences was not very deep. Still the work initiated by Sir Syed Ahmad Khan deserves our praise. In any case the advances in scientific knowledge in the present century made the task of reconstructing religious thought in Islam most imperative. As remarked by Iqbal:—

"The task before the modern Muslim is, therefore, immense. He has to rethink the whole system of Islam without completely breaking with the past. Perhaps the first Muslim who felt the urge of a new spirit in him was Shah Wali Ullah of Delhi. The man, however, who fully realized the importance and immensity of the task, and whose deep insight into the inner meaning of the history of Muslim thought and life, combined with a broad vision engendered by his wide experience of men and manners, would have made him a living link between the past and the future, was Jamal-ud-Din Afghani. If his indefatigable but divided energy could have devoted itself entirely to Islam as a system of human belief and conduct, the world of Islam, intellectually speaking, would have been on a much more solid ground today. The only course open to us is to approach modern knowledge with a respectful but independent attitude and to appreciate the teachings of Islam in the light of that knowledge, even though we may be led to differ from those who have gone before us."*

*The Reconstruction of Religious Thought in Islam, Oxford University Press, p. 92,

Describing the impact of modern Western thought on Islam Iqbal says:—

"The most remarkable phenomenon of modern history, however, is the enormous rapidity with which the world of Islam is spiritually moving towards the West. There is nothing wrong in this movement, for European culture, on its intellectual side, is only a further development of some of the most important phases of the culture of Islam. Our only fear is that the dazzling exterior of European culture may arrest our movement and we may fail to reach the true inwardness of that culture. During all the centuries of our intellectual stupor Europe has been seriously thinking on the great problems in which the philosophers and scientists of Islam were so keenly interested. Since the Middle Ages, when the schools of Muslim theology were completed, infinite advance has taken place in the domain of human thought and experience. The extension of man's power over nature has given him a new faith and a fresh sense of superiority over the forces that constitute his environment. New points of view have been suggested, old problems have been re-stated in the light of fresh experience, and new problems have arisen. It seems as if the intellect of man is outgrowing its own most fundamental categories—time, space, and casualty. With the advance of scientific thought even our concept of intelligibility is undergoing a change. The theory of Einstein has brought a new vision of the universe and suggests new ways of looking at the problems common to both religion and philosophy. No wonder then that the younger generation of Islam in Asia and Africa demand a fresh orientation of their faith. With the reawakening of Islam, therefore, it is necessary to examine, in an indepedent spirit, what Europe has thought and how far the conclusions reached by her can help us in the revision and, if necessary, reconstruction, of theological thought in Islam".*

Iqbal undertook the great task of reconstructioning religious thought in Islam in the course of lectures that he was invited to deliver

*The Reconstruction of Religious Though t in Islam, p. 7.

at Madras, Hyderabad and Aligarh. These lectures have now been published in a volume called "The Reconstruction of Religious Thought in Islam." At one time Iqbal wanted to call the collection "Islam as I understand it". In these lectures Iqbal has discussed the fundamental principles of Islam in the light of modern thought and scientific knowledge and has at times reinterpreted some of the tenets.

The first lecture is entitled *Knowledge and Religious Experience*, and in this Iqbal discusses the difference between knowledge gained from various sources. The Quran, recognising the fact that the empirical attitude is an indispensable stage in the spiritual life of humanity, attaches equal importance to all the regions of human experience as yielding knowledge of the ultimate Reality, which reveals itself in symbols both within and without. To secure a complete vision of Reality sense—perception must be supplemented by the perception of what the Quran describes as *Qalb* or heart.

Describing the importance of religious experience to knowledge, Iqbal discusses the importance of intuition, which occupies such an important place in his philosophy. According to Iqbal, thought and intuition are not hostile to each other.

And for the purposes of knowledge, the region of mystic experience is as real as any other region of human experience, and cannot be disregarded just because it cannot be traced to sense-perception. The main characteristics of mystic experience are:—

(*i*) This experience is immediate.

(*ii*) This experience constitutes an unanalysable whole.

(*iii*) To the mystic the mystic state is a moment of intimate association with a unique other Self, transcending, encompassing and momentarily suppressing the private personality of the subject of experience.

(*iv*) Since the quality of the mystic experience is to be directly experienced, it cannot be communicated.

(*v*) The mystic's intimate association with the eternal, which gives him a sense of the unreality of serial time, does not mean a complete break with serial time.

As religious experience is essentially a state of feeling with a cognitive aspect, the content of which cannot be communicated to others except in the form of a judgement, the question naturally arises as to what is the guarantee of its truth. According to Iqbal we are in possession of tests which do not differ from those applicable to other forms of knowledge. These tests are intellectual and pregmatic. The former are applied by philosophers and the latter by prophets.

In the course of his second lecture entitled *The Philosophical Tests of Religious Experience* Iqbal deals with the intellectual tests which can be applied to religious experience. Thus it will be seen that religious experience is also subject to tests similar to those applicable to other forms of knowledge.

In his third lecture *The Conception of God and the Meaning of Prayer*, Iqbal elucidates Quranic conception of God, the important elements in which, from a purely intellectual point of view, are creativeness, knowledge, omnipotence, and Eternity. In the course of this lecture—Iqbal comments on the description of God as light, and his remarks are highly instructive and interesting, "Personally, I think the description of God as light, in the revealed literature of Judaism, Christianity, and Islam must now be interpreted differently. The teaching of modern physics is that the velocity of light cannot be exceeded and is the same for all observers whatever their own system of movement, Thus, in the world of change, light is the nearest approach to the Absolute. The metaphor of light as applied to God, therefore, must, in view of modern knowledge, be taken to suggest the Absoluteness of God and not His Omnipresence which easily lends itself to a pantheistic interpretation."* Iqbal conceives the

*The Reconstruction of Religious Thought in Islam, p. 61.

ultimate Reality as Ego, and from the ultimate Ego, only egos proceed only so far as creativeness is concerned. The world in all its details, from the mechanical movement of what we call the atom of matter to the free movement of thought in human ego, is the self-revelation of the "Great I am". Every atom of Divine energy, however low in the scale of existence, is an ego.

Religion is not satisfied with mere conception; it seeks a more intimate knowledge of an association with the object of its pursuit. The agency through which this association is achieved is the art of worship or prayer. Prayer as a means of spiritual illumination is a normal vital act by which the little island of our personality suddenly discovers its situation in a larger whole of life. Iqbal says: "The truth is that all search for knowledge is essentially a form of prayer." The scientific observer of Nature is a kind of mystic seeker in the act of prayer. What a noble thought to regard scientific research as a form of prayer. The real object of prayer, however, is better achieved when the act of prayer becomes congregational. The spirit of all prayer is essentially social. Prayer, whether individual or associative is an expression of man's inner yearning for a response in the awful silence of the universe. "From the unity of the all-inclusive Ego who creates and sustains all egos, follows the essential unity of all mankind. The division of mankind into races, nations, and tribes, according to the Quran, is for purposes of identification only. The Islamic form of association in prayer, therefore, besides its cognitive value, is further indicative of the aspiration to realize this essential unity of mankind as a fact in life by demolishing all barriers which stand between man and man."*

In his fourth lecture, Iqbal deals with *The Human Ego, His Freedom and Immortality*. We have already dealt with the human ego in a previous chapter. But in this lecture Iqbal explains among other things how, with all the insistence that Islam lays on the freedom of the ego, the most degrading type of Fatalism came to prevail in

*The Reconstruction of Religious Thought in Islam, p. 89.

the world of Islam. According to Iqbal the kind of Fatalism which the European critics sum up in the word *Qismat* was due partly to philosophical thought, partly to political expedience, and partly to the gradually diminishing force of the life-impulse which Islam originally imparted to its followers. Referring to the type of Fatalism prevalent in the world of Islam, Iqbal writes:—

"Thus arose, in spite of open protests by Muslim divines, a morally degarding Fatalism, and the constitutional theory known as the accomplished fact in order to support vested interests. This is not at all surprising. In our own times philosophers have furnished a kind of intellectual justification for the finality of the present capitalistic structure of society. Hegel's view of Reality as an infinitude of reason from which follows the essential rationality of the real, and Augustus Comtes' society as an organism in which specific functions are eternally assigned to each organ, are instances in point. The same thing appears to have happened in Islam. But since Muslims have always sought the justification of their varying attitudes in the Quran, even though at the expense of its plain meaning, the fatalistic interpretation has had very far-reaching effects on Muslim peoples."*

In the fifth lecture, Iqbal deals with the *Spirit of Muslim Culture*. According to the Quran the inner experience is only one source of human knowledge, the other two sources being Nature and History; and it is in tapping all these sources of knowledge that the spirit of Islam is seen at its best. According to Iqbal Greek, thought in no way determined the character of Muslim culture. The cultural value of a great idea in Islam—the finality of the institution of prophethood is not fully appreciated. According to Iqbal in Islam prophecy reaches its perfection in discovering the need of its abolition. In order to achieve full self-consciousness it is necessary that man must finally be thrown back on his own resources. The abolition of priesthood and hereditary kingship in Islam, the constant appeal to reason and experience in the Quran, and the importance it attaches to Nature

***The Reconstruction of Religious Thought in Islam, p. 105.**

and History as sources of human knowledge, are all different aspects of the same idea of finality.

The most important characteristic of Muslim culture is insistence on a dynamic conception of the universe. It is one of the most essential teachings of the Quran that nations are collectively judged and suffer for their misdeeds here and now. In order to establish this proposition the Quran constantly cites historical instances and urges upon the reader to reflect on the past and present experiences of mankind. Two ideas form the basis of the Quranic teachings in this connections:—

(1) The unity of human origin. "And we have created you all from one breath of life."
(2) A keen sense of the reality of time, and the concept of life as continuous movement in time.

If the true significance of these basic principles is borne in mind by the intellectual and spiritual leaders of mankind, the world will be a different place to live in.

The sixth lecture deals with *The Principle of Movement in the Structure of Islam*. As already remarked the Islamic view of the universe is fundamentally dynamic. It rejects blood-relationship as a basis of human unity. The search for a purely psychological foundation of human unity becomes possible only with the perception that all human life is spirtual in origin. Islamic culture finds the foundation of world unity in the principle of '*Tauhid*'. The ultimate spiritual basis of all life, as conceived by Islam, is eternal and reveals itself in variety and change. A society organised on such a basis must reconcile in its life the categories of permanence and change. But eternal principles when they are understood to exclude all possibilities of change, tend to immobilise what is essentially mobile in nature. The principle of movement in the structure of Islam is *Ijtihad*, and it is a great pity that this life-giving principle was never allowed to operate freely among the Muslims. Among the various causes that led to the decline of the Muslim people neglect of *Ijtihad* was one of the most important.

In this lecture Iqbal has also stressed the importance of *Ijma* as a source of Muslim Law. Iqbal says: "The third source of Mohammedan Law is *Ijma* which is, in my opinion perhaps the most important legal notion in Islam. It is, however, strange that this important notion, while invoking great academic discussion in early Islam, remained practically a mere idea, and rarely assumed the form of a permanent institution in any Mohammedan country. Possibly its transformation into a permanent legislative institution was contrary to the political interests of the kind of absolute monarchy that grew up in Islam immediately after the fourth Caliph. It was, I think, favourable to the interest of the Omayyad and the Abbaside Caliphs to leave the power of *Ijtihad* to individual *Mujtahids* rather than encourage the formation of a permanent assembly which might become too powerful for them. It is, however, extremely satisfactory to note that the pressure of new world forces and the political experience of European nations are impressing on the mind of modern Islam the value and possibilities of the idea of *Ijma*. The growth of republican spirit, and the gradual formation of legislative assemblies in Muslim lands constitutes a great step in advance. The transfer of the power of *Ijtihad* from individual representative of schools to a Muslim legislative assembly which, in view of the growth of opposing sects, is the only possible form *Ijma* can take in modern times, will secure contributions to legal discussion from laymen who happen to possess a keen insight into affairs."*

The subject of the last lecture is: *Is Religion possible*? This is a fundamental question affecting mankind generally, especially today, when the whole world is looking for a fundamental principle on which to build up human accord and peace. It is impossible to improve upon the language that Iqbal employs to answer this question. Iqbal says:—

*The Reconstruction of Religious Thought in Islam, p. 164.

"And religion, which in its higher manifestations is neither dogma, nor priesthood, nor ritual, can alone ethically prepare the modern man for the burden of the great responsibilty which the advancement of modern science necessarily involves and restore to him that attitude of faith which makes him capable of winning a personality here and retaining it hereafter. It is only by rising to a fresh vision of his origin and future, his whence and whither, that man will eventually triumph over a society motivated by an inhuman competition, and a civilization which has lost its spiritual unity by its inner conflict of religious and political values."[1]

The truth is that the religious and the scientific processes, though involving different methods, are identical in their final aim. Actually religion is more anxious to attain the Real than science.

We have given above a brief summary of the numerous subjects and problems dealt by Iqbal in his seven lectures. The nature of the subjects dealt with and the philosophical method of dealing with them render any attempt to summarise beset with numerous difficulties. Some of these difficulties have been overcome by quoting profusely from Iqbal himself. In most cases it was found impossible to improve upon the language used by Iqbal. From what has been said above the supreme importance of the questions touched by Iqbal in these lectures should be obvious. When dealing with these subjects Iqbal brought to bear on them a profound knowledge of Islamic thought, an intensive study of the Quran, an uptodate knowledge of Western thought and sciences, along with great originality of thought. There was no man better qualified to deal with the subjects than Iqbal, and the world in general, and the Islamic people in particular, owe a deep debt of gratitude to Iqbal for having shown them the way in which the principle of movement must be allowed to operate in the religious thought if humanity is to solve the various spiritual and moral problems that are confronting it today. Many writers regard Iqbal as the ablest exponent of the rationalistic movement

[1] The Reconstruction of Religious Thought in Islam, p. 178.

in Islam known as ***Jadid Ilm-i-Kalam***. This he was, but saying that does not fully describe the true significance of his great work. By his original thinking Iqbal not only shook the stagnation which had obstructed all growth in Islamic thought for centuries, but also revealed for the first time the true spiritual and moral significance of some of the basic teachings. He established for the first time the connection between these teachings and the development of society. Before his death Iqbal was deeply interested in the question whether the Law of Islam is capable of evolution. In order to demonstrate that it is so, he wanted to write a book "*The Reconstruction of Muslim Jurisprudence*". He had collected a large number of books for this purpose and had even prepared some notes. It is hoped that a team of research workers will be able to complete this work. Even in the realm of religious thought Iqbal was only able to indicate the general lines on which the reconstruction must proceed, and it is our duty to carry on the great work initiated by him with unabated enthusiasm and painstaking research, because new situations are arising everyday due to advances in human knowledge. As remarked by Iqbal: "It must however, be remembered that there is no such thing as finality in philosophical thinking. As knowledge advances and fresh avenues of thought are opened, other views, and probably sounder views than those set forth in these lectures are possible. Our duty is carefully to watch the progress of human thought, and to maintain an independent critical attitude towards it."

SIX

Iqbal in Foreign Lands

EVERY student of Iqbal knows that the universal appeal of his poetry and philosophy lies in the fact that, like Goethe, he is a seer and a humanist. In view of this fact, it is not surprising that Iqbal is not only popular in countries where Urdu and Persian—the two languages in which he wrote poetry—are understood, but also wherever translations of his poetry are available. In this connection an account of circumstances under which he received his knighthood would be found interesting. Sometime in 1920, there arrived at Government House, Lahore, a European traveller, and he expressed a desire to meet Iqbal. The Governor of the Punjab asked his guest as to how he had come to know about Iqbal. Thereupon the guest replied that he had heard people in Central Asia reciting Iqbal's poems.

Iqbal's Persian poems reached Afghanistan quite early because the cultural relations of that country with the Punjab and certain other parts of Pakistan were always intimate. Moreover Iqbal had dedicated his *Payam-i-Mashriq* to Amanullah, the ill-fated king of Afghanistan. When there was turmoil in that country and Amanullah had to flee with his family it was left to General Nadir Khan, later on known as Nadir Shah, to restore order in that country, and Iqbal met the General at Lahore Railway Station when he was on his way to Kabul. It is said that the troubles in Afghanistan had affected Iqbal so much that he offered General Nadir Khan a considerable sum of money to help him in his mission. It is not known whether the General accepted that sum of money or not, but he always entertained great esteem for the poet, and in 1933 he invited Iqbal to visit Afghanistan. On return from Afghanistan, Iqbal composed a poem

The Traveller in which he recorded his impression of Afghanistan, and gave some sound advice to King Zahir Shah who had, by the time the poem was composed, succeeded his father who was killed by an assassin.

During his stay in Kabul, Iqbal was entertained by several local societies and glowing tributes were paid to him as the poet-prophet of the East.

Sardar Salahuddin Seljuki, who used to be Consul-General for Afghanistan in Delhi for many years and later on in Karachi, was a great friend of Iqbal. Whenever Iqbal visited Delhi he always stayed with Salahuddin Seljuki.

Salahuddin wrote several illuminating articles on Iqbal's message and poetry. These have been published in the form of a book. When Iqbal died, the Government of Afghanistan sent a beautiful marble tombstone for his grave.

Iqbal was little read in Iran until late in the thirties and it was left to the Persian Poet-Laureate, Bahar Khorasani, to introduce Iqbal to the Iranians. In his great work of literary criticism entitled "Sabk-Shinasi", Bahar has devoted a separate chapter to what he calls Iqbal's School of Poetry. Bahar has also paid great tribute to the greatness of Iqbal in a poem written by him.

Other writers in Iran have also written poems and articles on Iqbal, and Dr. Mujtaba Minavi has written a book called "Iqbal Lahori". Another collection of essays on Iqbal by many leading writers of Iran was published by the journal 'Danish' under the name of "Iqbal Namah". Today Iqbal is widely read in Iran and it can be said that his philosophy and poetry are both highly appreciated in that country.

It is true that Iqbal himself wanted his poetry to reach as wide a circle of humanity as was possible, and that was one of the many reasons why he took to writing in Persian. When a scholar asked

Iqbal as to why he started writing poetry in Persian in preference to Urdu, his reply was very significant. Iqbal said: "Because I could not write in Arabic, so I took to Persian." At that time little did Iqbal know that his works will reach the Arab-speaking world through excellent translations which would possess all the glory and majesty of the original. Some of the earliest introductions that Iqbal got to the Arab world were through "Al-Bashir"—the Arabic magazine of Pakistan. Hasan-al-Azami, a Pakistani, published Arabic translations of some of Iqbal's poems, especially his *Tarana-i-Milli* in the Arabic journal. Hasan-al-Azami also brought out an anthology entitled "Iqbal's Philosophy", prepared in collaboration with a prominent Egyptian poet, Saidy Aly Shablan, whose translation of *Shikwa* and *Jawab Shikwa* were included in the collection. Later on another anthology of Arabic translation of Iqbal's poems was published in Baghdad which contained translations by the Iraqi poetess Amina Nureddin. But it was left to that great Arabic *litterateur*—Dr. Abdul Wahab Azzam to introduce Iqbal to the Arab world. Dr. Abdul Wahab Azzam is not only a linguist, but also a great scholar, a philosopher and a poet of high order. He has a wounderful and at times uncanny capacity of rendering into Arabic poems from different languages. Dr. Azzam had translated portions of Rumi's *Mathnawi*. His translations are characterised by such eloquence, spontaneity and felicity of expression that they read like original poetry of a high order. Dr. Azzam was Professor of Persian at Al-Azhar University before coming to Pakistan and his knowledge of Persian language and literature was profound. So the first book he translated was *Payam-i-Mashriq*. During his stay in Karachi, he learnt Urdu and then he translated Iqbal's *Zarb-i-Kaleem*. Translation of *Payam-i-Mashriq* was published by the Iqbal Society, Karachi, and that of *Zarb-i-Kaleem* by the Cultural Society of Al-Azhar University. Lately he has translated *Ashrar-o-Rumuz* This translation is already in the press and will be out soon.

All these translations by Dr. Azzam, besides introducing Iqbal to the Arab world, are in themselves a contribution to modern Arabic poetry.

Iqbal is becoming popular in Turkey also. Recently a brochure was published by "La Turquie Moderne", Istanbul, entitled "Rumi and Iqbal". *Payam-i-Mashriq* has been translated in Turkish by Dr. Ali Ganjeli.

In Indonesia, Mr. Bahrum Rangkuti translated several of his poems and the collection was published by Messrs. Almarco. After publishing this collection he translated *Asrar-i-Khudi* which has been published by Messrs. Balai Pustaka. A collection of articles on Iqbal by leading literary figures of Indonesia has been published in a special number of the well-known magazine "Abian Islam" (September, 1952).

Turning now to the Western languages, the first translation of importance was of Iqbal's poem *Asrar-i-Khudi* by Dr. R. A. Nicholson of Cambridge in 1920. This translation was originally published by Messrs. Macmillan & Co., of London. The second edition of this translation was considerably improved in accordance with Iqbal's suggestions. Dr. Nicholson was eminently qualified to translate Iqbal as he was a life-long student of Rumi and so was able to probe into the inner working of Iqbal's mind. His translations of Rumi's *Mathnawi* and *Diwan Shams-i-Tabrez* were declared by all scholars as masterpieces. Dr. Nicholson had the further advantage of referring all difficult points to Iqbal himself for clarification.

After translating *Asrar-i-Khudi*, Dr. Nicholson wrote several articles on Iqbal, especially in the "Islamica", and translated stray poems. But the next translation of any importance was of the quatrains contained in *Payam-i-Mashriq* by Professor A. J. Arberry. This translation was in verse and was known as *Tulips of Sinai*. This was followed by Arberry's translation of the *Ghazals* of *Zabur-i-Ajam*, under the title *Persian Psalms*; it was published by Ashraf, of Lahore.

The next translation to appear was a collection of poems taken entirely from his Urdu works. This was *Poems of Iqbal* by

V. G. Kiernan, published by Kutub Publishers, Bombay. This is a remarkable book of translations from Iqbal as it gives a complete picture of the development of Iqbal's poetic genius in Urdu. The author has tried to copy not only the rhyme scheme but even the metre of the original. Some translations are simply superb.

Shikwa and *Jawab-i-Shikwa* were translated by Mr. Altaf Husain in English verse and the translation was published by Ashraf, of Lahore, under the title 'Complaint and Answer'. Similarly *Khizr-i-Rah* has been translated by A. Q. Niaz and published by Friends in Counsel Publishers, Lahore. Mention must be made here of a translation of *Rumuz-i-Bekhudi* by Professor A. J. Arberry that is being published by John Murray of London.

It is not proposed to attempt a critical evaluation of the translators mentioned above, but it will be seen that the English-speaking world has now sufficient material to enjoy Iqbal's great art. Translating poetry written in one language into another is not an easy task, and it is a moot point whether such translations should be in prose or verse. There is no doubt that the restrictions of versification add to the difficulties of translation. When mentioning this we cannot forget the success attained by Fitzgerald in translating Omar Khayyam but the liberties taken by Fitzgerald cannot be permitted in any translation claiming accuracy. In the introduction to his translation of *Diwan Shams-i-Tabrez*, Prof. R. A. Nicholson says:

> "My translation seems to reconcile the claims of accuracy and art: it is therefore in prose."

As regards translation of Iqbal's poems in other European languages, Professor Hell, of Erlangen University had translated quotations of *Payam-i-Mashriq* in German, but he died before the translations could be published. These translations are with Professor Annemarie Schimmel, of Marburg, now, and it is hoped that they will be published soon. Moreover Professor Schimmel has written a series of illuminating articles on Iqbal.

Madame Eva Meyerovitch of Paris has translated Iqbal's *Reconstruction of Religious Throught in Islam* in French and is busy translating *Development of Metaphysics in Persia.* While translating these books this lady was so impressed by Iqbal's thought that she is now studying Persian so as to be able to translate *Zabur-i-Ajam* in French. It is a pity that no translations of Iqbal's poems in French have been published so far. But in Italy Iqbal has attained great popularity. A young Italian scholar, Professor Alessandro Bausani has made a complete translation of Iqbal's *Javid Namah*, into Italian under the name "Il Poema Celeste" which is published by the Institute Italiano Per II Medio ed Estremo Oriente. The fact that the first European language in which *Javid Namah* has been translated is Italian, is remarkable, because there is no doubt that it was a study of the researches of Miguel Asin on the influence that some Arab writers exercised on Dante in writing his "Divina Commedia" that really encouraged Iqbal to write this poem.

Iqbal himself was very keen to see a translation of *Javid Namah* in a European language published with illustrations. Now that a superb translation has already seen the light of the day, it is hoped that an illustrated edition will be brought out soon.

Thus it will be seen that even those unacquainted with Urdu and Persian have ample opportunity of reading Iqbal in translations today. In making Iqbal accessible to the Western world, Cambridge has played a great part through Nicholson and Arberry. This is but apt as Iqbal was a Cambridge man. In the end mention must be made of the great interest in Iqbal and his work that is being taken in the United States of America especially at Yale University, under the guidance of Professor F. S. C. Northrop.

Works of Iqbal

A. POETRY

(In Urdu)

1. "Bang-i-Dara", 1924.
2. "Bal-i-Jibrail", 1935.
3. "Zarb-i-Kalim", 1937.

(In Persian)

1. "Asrar-i-Khudi", 1915.
2. "Rumuz-i-Bekhudi", 1918.
3. "Payam-i-Mashriq", 1923.
4. "Zabur-i-Ajam", 1929.
5. "Javid-Namah", 1932.
6. "Musafir", 1934.
7. "Pas Chai Bayad Kard", 1936.
8. "Armughan-i-Hijaz" (Published posthumously).

B. PROSE

(*In English*)

1. "The Development of Metaphysics in Persia", Luzac & Co London, 1908.
2. "The Reconstruction of Religious Thought in Islam" (Oxford University Press, 1934).
3. "Letters of Iqbal to Jinnah", (Ashraf, Lahore, 1944).
4. "Speeches and Statements of Iqbal". (Al-Manar Academy, Lahore, 1944).

TRANSLATIONS OF IQBAL'S WORKS

(*In English*)

1. "Secrets of the Self" by R.A. Nicholson. Published by Ashraf, Lahore, 1920.
2. "Tulips of Sinai" by A. J. Arberry. Published by The Royal India Society, London, 1947.
3. "Poems from Iqbal" by V.G. Kiernan. Published by Kutub Publishers Ltd., Bombay, 1947.
4. "Persian Psalms" by A.J. Arberry (Ashraf, Lahore) 1948.
5. "Complaint and Answer" by Altaf Husain. (Ashraf, Lahore) 1943.

Books on Iqbal

(*In English*)

"Iqbal: His Poetry and Message" by Sheikh Akbar Ali (Qaumi Kutub Khana, Lahore) 1932.

"Aspects of Iqbal" (Qaumi Kutub Khana, Lahore) 1938.

"The Poet of the East" by Abdulla Anwar Beg, (Qaumi Kutub Khana, Lahore) 1930.

"Iqbal's Philosophy of Society" and "A study in Iqbal's Philosophy" by B.A. Dar, (Sh. Mohd. Ashraf, Lahore) 1933 and 1944 respectively.

"Metaphysics of Iqbal" by Dr. Ishrat Hasan Enver. (Sh. Mohd. Ashraf, Lahore) 1944.

"Iqbal As a Thinker" (Sh. Mohd. Ashraf, Lahore) 1944.

"A Voice from the East" by Zulfiqar Ali Khan (The Mercantile Electric Press, Lahore) 1922.

"Iqbal" by Roop Krishna (New India Publications, Lahore) 1945.

"Iqbal's Educational Philosophy" by K.G. Saiyidain, (Sh. Mohd. Ashraf, Lahore) 1938.

"Iqbal: The Poet and His Message" by Sachchindananda Sinha, (Ram Narain Lal, Allahabad) 1946.

"Iqbal: His Art and Thought" by S. A. Vahid, (Sh. Mohd. Ashraf, Lahore) 1944.

www.ingramcontent.com/pod-product-compliance
Lightning Source LLC
Chambersburg PA
CBHW062147160726
48282CB00027B/947